complete leadership

COMPLETE LEADERSHIP

a practical guide for
developing your
leadership talents

Susan Bloch
&Philip Whiteley

www.yourmomentum.com
the stuff that drives you

managers

Manager's momentum – a new suite of management development books for the leaders of the future

We've taken the successful approach of the momentum personal development books – active personal coaching, applied personal values and highly stimulating delivery – and applied it to the portfolio of skills that talented leaders of the future will want and need. The result? A set of books and accelerated learning tools for smart managers that will equip you for a bright future of managing talented people and entrepreneurial ventures.

These are intelligent, inspiring yet practical books on a new breed of essential managerial topics – a far cry from an older style of management book, which too often features the same old tired subjects drowned in dense text. Manager's momentum is characterized by edgy, modern subjects delivered in an easily absorbed dynamic style. These are books to make you energized, not tired. And books that you'll be happy to be seen with.

Other manager's momentum titles:

Managing talented people
getting on with – and getting the best from – your high performers
Alan Robertson and Graham Abbey

Solution-focused coaching
a manager's guide to getting the best from people
Tony Grant and Jane Greene

Also available – momentum personal development books for the stuff that drives you.

Lead yourself
be where others will follow
Mick Cope

Change activist
make big things happen fast
Carmel McConnell

Innervation
personal training for life and work
Guy Browning

The complete list of momentum personal development titles is available via
www.yourmomentum.com and **www.business-minds.com**

momentum prescription – Let Us Help You Work Out Which Book Will Suit Your Symptoms

Feel stuck in a rut? Something wrong and need help doing something about it?

◆ If you need tools to help make changes in your life: **coach yourself** (a good general guide to change)

◆ If you are considering dramatic career change: **snap, crackle or stop**

◆ If you need to work out what you'd like to be doing and how to get there: **be your own career consultant**

◆ If you need help making things happen and tackling the 'system' at work/in life: **change activist**

◆ If you think you want more from your life than a 'normal' career: **careers un-ltd**

Feel that you can never make decisions and you just let things 'happen'?

◆ If you need help making choices: **the big difference**

◆ If you want to feel empowered and start making things happen for yourself: **change activist**

Feel life is too complicated and overwhelming?

◆ If you need help working through office politics and complexity: **clued up**

◆ If you need a kick up the backside to get out of your commerce-induced coma: **change activist**

◆ If you need an amusing and very helpful modern life survival guide: **innervation**

◆ If you never have enough time or energy to get things done or think properly: **mental space**

Feel like you might be in the wrong job?

◆ If you want help finding your destiny job and inspiration to make that dramatic career change: **snap, crackle or stop**

◆ If you feel like you aren't doing a job that is really what you are about': **soultrader**

◆ If you are struggling with the 'do something worthwhile OR make money dilemma': **change activist**

◆ If you think you want more from your life than a 'normal' career: **careers un-ltd**

Feel that you're not the person/leader you should be?

◆ If you want to be the kind of person others want to follow: **lead yourself**

◆ If you feel your working relationships with people could improve: **managing yourself**

◆ If you need help becoming the person you've always wanted to be: **reinvent yourself**

◆ If you want to work out everything you've got to offer, and how to improve that: **grow your personal capital**

Feel you need help getting your ideas into action?

◆ If the problem is mainly other people, lack of time and the messiness of life: **clued up**

◆ If the problem is communicating your thinking: **hey you!**

◆ If the problem is getting things across to other people: **managing yourself**

◆ If the problem is more ideas than time and you are a bit overwhelmed with work: **mental space**

◆ If the problem is making change in your life: **coach yourself**

Feel you aren't projecting yourself and managing your career as well as you should?

◆ If you'd like to be the kind of person people think of first: **managing brand me**

◆ If you'd like people to listen to your ideas more readily: **hey you!**

◆ If you'd like to come across as the person you really are inside: **soultrader**

◆ If you need general help in changing the way you work/live: **coach yourself**

◆ If you need help working out what you've got and how best to use it: **float you**

Feel you'd like to be much more creative and a real 'ideas person'

◆ If you need inspiration on how to be innovative and think creatively: **innervation**

◆ If you need help spreading your ideas and engendering support: **hey you!**

PEARSON EDUCATION LIMITED

Head Office
Edinburgh Gate
Harlow CM20 2JE
Tel: +44 (0)1279 623623
Fax: +44 (0)1279 431059

London Office:
128 Long Acre, London WC2E 9AN
Tel: +44 (0)20 7447 2000
Fax: +44 (0)20 7447 2170
Website: www.yourmomentum.com
        www.business-minds.com

First published in Great Britain in 2003

© Pearson Education Limited 2003

The right of Susan Bloch and Philip Whiteley to be identified as Authors of this Work has been asserted by them in accordance with the Copyright, Designs and Patents Act 1988.

ISBN 1843 04025 5

British Library Cataloguing in Publication Data
A CIP catalogue record for this book can be obtained from the British Library.

10 9 8 7 6 5 4 3 2 1

Typeset by Northern Phototypesetting Co. Ltd, Bolton
Printed and bound in Great Britain by Henry Ling Ltd, Dorchester

The Publishers' policy is to use paper manufactured from sustainable forests.

Thank you...

We acknowledge the time and assistance that was given by all those who collaborated with us to make this book so immediate and relevant. Their sharing of their real life experiences has helped to shape our thinking. In particular, Gerry Robinson, Sue Turner, Barbara Moorhouse, Ian Carlisle, Greg Lewin, Dave Bennett, Claire Hall-Moore and Andy Parfitt, who provided us with open and frank one-to-one interviews.

We would like to thank Daniel Goleman for his support, and the Hay Group for giving us access to the research papers.

Susan Bloch

To my children, Allon and Shelley, who have been my coaches and my constant inspiration, and to my husband John, who has provided challenging insights, as well as much needed humour.

Philip Whiteley

To my wife Rose, for her love, inspiration and support during the writing of this book.

contents

foreword

In my travels as a lecturer and consultant on leadership, I find the most common question I'm asked is, 'Can leadership be learned?'

I've spent half a decade looking into that very question, as a result of the data that showed emotional intelligence to be crucial in what sets apart the best leaders from the mediocre. I've done this work with my colleague, Richard Boyatzis, professor of organizational behaviour at the Weatherhead School of Management at Case Western Reserve University.

Both Boyatzis and myself date our interest in the question to our graduate school days at Harvard University, studying with the late Professor David McClelland. He, more than anyone, was responsible for taking the focus in evaluating the active ingredients of leadership away from the matters of background and pedigree, academic achievement and performance on intellectual tests. Instead, he proposed that organizations identify the set of capabilities that distinguish outstanding leaders from those who are just average – and hire, promote, and develop people for those capabilities.

Using a massive amount of such data from organizations of all kinds worldwide, Boyatzis and I have been able to identify both the specific set of abilities that are the active ingredients in great leadership, and the principles of learning that must be applied in order for learning to bring lasting improvement to a leader's repertoire. Those are the principles we set forth in our book *The New Leaders*, co-authored with Annie McKee.

In doing this work, we have benefited greatly from the co-operation of colleagues at the Hay Group, who themselves have been tilling these same fields for years, many of them working directly with David McClelland himself. Now I'm delighted that Susan Bloch, formerly of the Hay Group, has teamed up with Phil Whiteley to write this practical application of the best principles for cultivating new strengths in the competencies that make for great leadership.

My hope is that this will make such learning widely available, and that many people – leaders and those who follow alike – will benefit.

Daniel Goleman

introduction

Researchers from the University of Texas once asked a man in casual dress to cross a busy city street in violation of the 'WAIT' pedestrian signal. Very few people followed. Then they asked a well-groomed man in a suit to do the same. Dozens followed his lead.[1] The study concluded that the apparel of authority could increase the likelihood of people following someone's example by 350 per cent.

One should never underestimate the power of authority. In a business or a team that authority resides primarily with the manager or leader. Employees volunteer their time, and whether they follow the lead that's set depends enormously on the authority of the individual in charge. In turn, this depends on motivational qualities which are, of course, more three-dimensional and more complex than sartorial matters that might persuade strangers to cross the street.

This book assumes that you are a leader of a team or an organization, or that you are close to assuming such a post. Our starting point is that you have a powerful influence on your colleagues and staff, whether you recognize this or not; and that many business leaders and managers either do not recognize this or are unprepared for it. A study by Daniel Goleman, looking at 15 global companies, attributes 85–90 per cent of leadership success to emotional intelligence.

Most people reaching an executive position have had more formal training in technical disciplines than in the art of leading people. You may be an expert software developer, an accountant, a marketer or a start-up entrepreneur, but you quickly discover that the way in which you manage, motivate and negotiate with people is at least half your role. Yet, while your formal training in technical disciplines no doubt amounted to several years, training in people management skills often numbers just days or even hours, despite growing awareness of its importance.

We can enter an executive role believing that business is principally about objectives, structures and strategy. But we soon discover that our time is spent dealing with people. It's about relationships, not matrices or structures. No wonder such a high proportion of managers feel unprepared for a senior role – nearly half, according to a study of business leaders.[2]

The same paper showed that one of the biggest areas where leaders lack preparation is in handling people. Asked to define the skills and behaviours necessary for success, the most commonly cited on the list were 'influencing across organizational boundaries' and 'top team development'. In another survey nine out of ten managers considered people skills vital for business success, but only one-third of the sample reported that their employers were committed to helping them develop such abilities.[3] More than two-thirds of the respondents were working with five or more teams, across disciplines and organizational and geographical boundaries, often without direct authority.

This book aims to:

◆ **build** on your personal leadership skills and illustrate their strategic importance

◆ **equip** you with the people skills which, allied to your technical and market knowledge, make you the complete leader.

The book is a personal coaching manual, with guides and questionnaires that can be applied directly to the teams with which you are working. It is rooted in the latest research and in the real-life experience of what it takes to run an effective business, division or team. It relates some real stories of successful business leaders who have experienced and overcome these challenges.

Leadership is an increasingly challenging role. But it is not impossible, nor intangible, nor given only to a select few 'born' leaders. It is even measurable. This book sets out a programme for step-by-step improvement and offers a means by which you can gauge your progress.

Complete Leadership also seeks to inspire; to remind those at the top that what you do is worthwhile; to illustrate the connections between your personal development, the achievement of your team members and the improvements in the quality of life for the customers that you serve. We encourage you to let your personality and true qualities shine.

Many business leaders have long aspired to reach a position of influence. This is the time of your life. Enjoy it.

chapter one
they talk about you – how leadership affects the staff

Learning points from this chapter

◆ The behaviour of the boss has a huge impact on the team.

◆ Having outside interests keeps you rooted and balanced.

◆ It's only healthy to occasionally feel daunted by a challenge.

◆ Preparing for the top job is essential and includes working on interpersonal skills.

◆ Societal changes are altering the emphasis of some leadership skills.

◆ Female executives face extra pressures, but should resist the temptation to try to be 'superwoman'.

Everyone who works spends a part of their day talking about their boss. This ranges from the positive, 'She'll let me go on that executive programme and then I'll have the opportunity to go for the Hong Kong job,' to the quizzical, 'He spent ages on the phone again,' to the negative, 'You won't *believe* what he did this time!' Such snippets of everyday life appear to be the stuff of gossip; the froth that floats on corporate life, but they actually tell us a great deal about the ability of teams and organizations to succeed. Leadership style accounts for up to 70 per cent of difference in organizational climate, which in turn can make an improvement of up to 25 per cent in business performance, Hay Group research has shown.

In short, organizations where people think 'Great! The boss is in today!' do better than those where people think 'Oh no! He's back from holiday!' This doesn't mean that you, the leader, ought to be soft or indecisive – staff actually don't like that – but rather that you need to convey the rich tapestry of authoritativeness, empathy, decision-making and coaching ability that brings out the best in others and in yourself.

Crucially, this depends on how you behave, as well as how you think. It sounds like a simple step, but it can be a difficult one. It's analogous to the difference between reading about the Olympics and learning how to swim.

As Daniel Goleman, author of *Emotional Intelligence* notes, emotional or behavioural patterns are more deeply set and require more effort to change than knowledge-based patterns of thinking. We'll explore this some more in Chapter 6. It has also been convincingly illustrated that the behaviour of a boss actually affects the blood pressure of his or her team. Researchers at Buckinghamshire Chilterns University College concluded: 'Your boss could be damaging your health.' In a controlled experiment, the researchers measured the blood pressure of healthcare assistants who had two supervisors who worked on alternate days of the week. Those who had one boss they liked and one they did not had significantly higher blood pressure than a control group, who liked both their bosses. (*New Scientist*, 5 January 2002.)

Everybody has a boss. Few would argue that they are not important in their lives. And all of us can remember the boss from hell, as well as the boss who really helped us to transform our lives.

Think about who your boss really is, especially if you have more than one boss, or if you've had three new bosses over the last 16 months, or if you have a virtual boss.

All of us can remember the boss from hell, as well as the boss who really helped us to transform our lives.

Studies suggest that effective managers make the time and effort to build effective working relationships with their bosses.[4] However, many people today still have the expectation that it's their boss's job to manage them, and that they have no part to play in this relationship other than to be 'managed'. Where the relationship doesn't work, the boss is usually to blame, or it's simply assumed that when two people can't work together in a boss–subordinate relationship it's merely a case of 'personality conflict'. That lazy phrase, however, is often just an alibi for failing to work at a relationship and failing to improve both communication and self-awareness.

Many managers make unrealistic assumptions of their bosses. They assume their bosses will somehow know what help or information they need in order to do their job well. At the most senior levels there are still complaints of 'my boss doesn't compliment me,' or 'it's my boss's job to find out what's going on, not mine to tell him.'

We'll give more guidance on this in Chapter 9, under 'How to Manage Your Boss' (page 160).

Before discussing particular skills, we need to consider the contemporary context. The challenges of the modern world are formidable, so don't be surprised if you feel or have to confront some of what follows.

'What am I doing here? (Maybe I'm not up to it . . .?)'

There can be a sense of loss, even loneliness, when you reach a senior position. You may miss former colleagues, you might even feel their envy if you've been promoted within the same organization. In the study cited above[2] a surprising proportion – nearly one-third of the sample – reported that they had sometimes regretted moving to a senior post. When asked 'What do you miss about your previous role?' nearly half the sample reported that they had sometimes missed 'company culture', 'familiarity with old role' and 'office location/environment'. Only around one in five respondents said that they had never missed such features.

The feeling of isolation was expressed by one individual who had recently become a partner at a new firm:

'The little things – where stuff is filed, parking, how to program the mobile. Cultural differences intensified by the fact that I moved from being employee to owner. I don't know which colleagues I can automatically turn to for help; I don't know who I can trust.'[5]

Even the great and the good went through this phase. Gerry Robinson, former chief executive of leisure and media giant Granada, reached a senior post at Coca-Cola in his late 20s. He recalls:

'I hated it because it's the first time that you move out from a group of peers. At any other level, even when you're on a board, you are still part of a group of other people. I hated the move away – it is very separating. I found it very tough and it took me quite a long time to realize that you couldn't change it very much. However easy you were; however relaxed you behaved, people were going to treat you differently if they reported to you. There is nothing you can do about it. I guess it's at that point that you really decide if this is for you or not. If it is, then it's going to get more and more distant as things move on so it's important to get your head around that.

'Equally, it is very very important at that stage to have other interests, because there are situations; whether it's your family, or golf or any other sport; anything else that you do that gives you normal relationships, with friends. That is really, really important, because from that moment on you are not going to have the normal cut and thrust of genuine one-to-one, balanced conversations with other people who work with you. It is simply not going to happen.'

Hearteningly, even Gerry Robinson admits that at times he has asked himself, 'Am I up to this?' The truth is, if we don't ask ourselves this, we are probably not attempting anything that stretches us, or anything worthwhile; or we are not being honest with ourselves. Think of it as a healthy instinct, not a symptom of weakness.

Mr Robinson continues:

'I've had this feeling lots of times. It occurs when you are taking on something new. I remember at Granada – I can't believe I was so stupid. I went into Granada having analyzed it every possible way in terms of its numbers. I thought: "There's such a lot you can do with this thing." It had to be capable of being turned around and being turned around quite quickly. But I never realized that this was something in the media that was going to be receiving all kinds of attention. At the time I ended up having to fire the chief executive of the television business; and the world collapsed around me. People were asking: "How can you do that to the poor guy?" I had absolutely no idea that it was going to be so public. It suddenly went through the roof. There have been lots of times when I've thought, "Oh, I hope I've got this right." Lots of times. And lots of times when it has taken me longer than I thought it would do. There have been times when I've got it wrong – thought I had got the right answer only to realize that it wasn't right. The capacity to say, "Just got it wrong – so change it; let's do it differently," is important. If you haven't got some doubts; if you think you know it all, then you are kidding yourself.'

Many executives find the long working hours that generally accompany a senior post debilitating. They have given up tennis or football, or riding or opera singing, or whatever their favourite pastime was. They rue the time they missed with their children as they grew up, and later ask themselves if it was all worth it. In early 2002 Danny O'Neil, chief executive of the UK financial services business group Britannic, announced he was standing down and taking up a three-day-a-week consulting role instead. The reason was that he wanted to spend more time with his children, including an 18-year-old daughter whom he felt he had missed too much as she grew up. Cynical voices immediately pounced on the familiar 'spending more time with his family' line and speculated as to the 'real' reasons for his departure. But even if there were other factors, they were unlikely to be significant given that he was actually staying with the group. More importantly there were commentators saying that his choice reflects the dilemmas that many people in middle life face.

'O'Neil is making a very significant life choice for himself and his family, one that will encourage lots of other highly stressed workaholics privately to reassess their own priorities. If I had a pound for every business man I've known down the years who has eventually confessed their greatest regret was not seeing their children grow up, I might even be able to afford to stop working myself. They are legion, believe me.'

Alf Young, *The Herald*, 18 January 2002

There are some fundamental, personal questions here that are difficult to air in a corporate setting. What is life for? Is this it? I say that the most important things in my life are my relationships and my children, so why do I arrange my life in such a way that I never see them?

You are not alone in feeling alone; you are not alone in trying to achieve the difficult balance of fulfilment at home and at work.

This book can't offer immediate solutions to these difficult choices. But we can tell you that you are not alone in feeling alone; that you are not alone in trying to achieve the difficult balance of fulfilment at home and at work. We aim to equip executives to manage time better, and to feel comfortable about confronting these matters, and we'll return to this theme in Chapter 6.

'I didn't realize how important it was to prepare for the top'

When Jeremy concluded the board meeting an hour later than scheduled he felt exhausted. There just seemed to be low energy in the executive team, and much cynical laughter. Why, he wondered, did the team tease David about his passion for fitness? David at least had run the Marathon in April and raised £5,000 for the blind dog association.

As he drove home he realized what a strain he had been under since moving into his new role four months previously: CEO of a major food retailer. He had wanted to run a business for years, and had come through the classic route of operations, marketing and strategy. Moving into the CEO role should have been easy. Why then was business slowing and growth in revenues dropping from 9 per cent to 4 per cent? He felt that he was under the microscope and constantly visible.

He realized, like many other managers – some 45 per cent, according to the survey quoted above[2] – that he hadn't really prepared himself for the role. Respondents to the survey who weren't prepared for their new role missed their old role more and were more likely to regret the move than those who had taken the time to understand the structures, culture and values in an organization. Like Jeremy, they missed old friendships and emotional support. It was hard not having those informal chats with his old team, and sharing some of the dramas of the day. Executives in the boardroom seemed so much more distant and unfriendly.

It was hard not having those informal chats with his old team, and sharing some of the dramas of the day.

Previously, as head of operations he'd had real clarity about what he was there to do. It was logistics and pricing, staffing and margins, and he had been really good at it. He'd struggled to find a strong person to replace him, perhaps the one thing he'd not been good at was finding a successor. No wonder the transition had been so difficult. He was still doing the operations job as well, as his replacement had only been in the job six weeks. The guy was going to take at least another two months until he got the hang of it.

Like 47 per cent of the respondents in the survey, Jeremy continued to work in a way that had served him well in the past. He often found himself thinking 'when I was head of ops . . .' Perhaps that was why one of the non-executive directors had pulled him aside over coffee and said, 'Jeremy, you need to begin to shine as the leader of this group. You're not just in charge of operations any more.'

By the time he reached home Jeremy, like many of the respondents to the survey (75 per cent) reflected that he felt only moderately satisfied with his achievements. His relationship with the chairman had got off to a very good start, but now appeared to be a bit rocky, and slower growth was certainly a worry. Perhaps he was not as clear as he should be about his role and goals. His predecessor had only been focused on cost-cutting and hadn't really paid much attention to succession planning or growth. Now there was nothing left to cut. Perhaps he had to start to think about changing ways rather than just cutting.

He arrived home, and tried to unwind as he showered, changed and began to relax. Some things were becoming a little clearer as he focused on nature of the daily challenges that confronted him, and the manner in which they differed from those he encountered as head of operations. His problems seemed to be about relationships and people skills – not something anyone had warned him of before his ascension to CEO. As head of operations there were more tasks and a more clearly defined role. Now his role was more like that of a politician; persuading, building constituencies and relating to people. No wonder he had found it tempting to slip back into a more task-focused role; perhaps the lack of experience of his replacement was just a cover for his tendency to interfere?

He began to realize what new skills and behaviours he needed in the job. He had to manage his relationship with the chairman and non-executive directors, and this was new to him. He was also required to meet with investors and journalists; another new role.

Above all, he had to develop a strong top team. It was time now to think about new ways of behaving. The question was how to do it all.

After months of struggle, however, fortune was about to take a kinder turn. He was in his office early the next morning. First visitor was his human resources director, a friendly, able individual whom Jeremy had not generally credited with prophetic powers, but who chose that very morning to suggest that he and the team explore the potential of coaching. The HR director's idea was that the top executives needed development to enable them to guide the transition of the business from its cost-focused phase to a more expansionist, outward-looking strategy. Like many executives (51 per cent in the survey reported above), Jeremy had never worked with a coach; in fact, the thought had never seriously entered his mind.

The answer he had been struggling for was a little closer. Initially, however, Jeremy felt deflated at the prospect; almost like a failure. After a few months struggling with the senior post, seeing revenues down, here was the HR guy suggesting an intervention that sounded almost like remedial training. He recalled also that in his last company his boss had had a coach and was fired four months later. He had a vaguely defined but powerful mental association between coaching and failure.

But he was also curious; recognizing that he had no idea really about what coaching was about. In the discussion with the HR director he realized that he needed to spend time reflecting on his new role; and, of course, just the evening before he had reached the conclusion that his political and interpersonal skills needed sharpening; if coaching did not help directly with that, it might at least inform his developmental needs more specifically.

He acknowledged that he should have taken time to stand back and understand the dynamics in the boardroom.

He acknowledged, like many others who move into new senior roles, that he should have taken time to stand back and understand the dynamics in the boardroom from the perspective of the leader rather than just a team member. He was now required to work more closely with his chairman to obtain greater clarity about what he and they were there to do. He thought about the stakeholder relationships; the prospect of debates and discussion with journalists and investors, and recognized that he had little experience in these areas. He decided that coaching could help him focus on developing skills such as adaptiveness, relationship management, and political awareness; but also that it was important to remain true to himself.

'Get real, Mum and Dad, this is the modern world'

Demographics and societal attitudes have changed sharply in recent decades. The people who work in organizations are different in number, lifestyle and attitude compared with previous decades, and some of the differences are profound. This affects the way leaders approach their role in ways that are only just beginning to be appreciated. Most of our business models are still descended from 100-year-old ideas of Frederick Taylor, who employed cloth-capped 'hands' to slot into the corporate machinery. The modern concept of people as 'human resources' is not much different, but in the 21st century people are free agents – often highly skilled and in short supply. Keeping them motivated and happy becomes a central concern.

We are tearing up 'command and control' structures, but not the 'command and control' mindsets.

As we noted earlier, many modern businesses feature complex team arrangements, joint ventures and temporary projects where a manager has high responsibility and accountability, but little direct authority over the people jointly responsible for meeting the targets. In general in business we are adding dramatically to the complexity of the people management tasks of managers, but we are not introducing the commensurate investment in development of the skills needed for such responsibilities. We are tearing up 'command and control' structures, but not the 'command and control' mindsets.

At a round-table discussion on managing international teams, hosted by Ashridge College, UK, in November 2001, one participant, Mary Kennedy, director of Ashridge College's 'Leading Complex Teams' programme, reported the following *cri de coeur* from a Japanese project manager working in Spain for a multinational company, heading a widely dispersed international team:

'My board is thinking that this is a new world, we can communicate instantly and work together and it is brilliant because we have a common vision, but I know that they are a bunch of prima donnas. Organizationally I am out on a limb: my career depends on getting these prima donnas to work together. My business does not think that it is difficult.'

This illustrates the complexity and challenge of handling people in the modern business, and how many businesses don't give the matter anywhere near the priority that it merits.

In most workplaces loyalty can't be demanded in the way that it might have been in the 1950s and 1960s, where corporations offered in reward the promise of a job for life. People change jobs more often than before. Although this trend has at times been exaggerated – a surprising number of people still stay with the same employer for more than 20 years – job-hopping is a feature of 21st century corporate life.

Some roots of attitudinal change lie outside the workplace – in education, mass media and youth culture. Whatever your view of the various generational theories concerning Baby Boomers, or Generation X, it's probably safe to conclude that people under 35 at the turn of the century are far less likely to be unquestioningly obedient towards authority figures than their parents, and certainly than their grandparents born during and before the Second World War. One can hear the refrain from many parents in middle age who comment: 'I would never have spoken to my parents the way my teenage daughter talks to me! She says things like "Get real, Dad!" I have to negotiate with her!' It's unlikely that the teenage daughter ceases to be so assertive when she enters the workforce. Her future bosses need to handle her carefully or she will work for the competitor.

Even demography has its impact on the importance of leadership. There are many more single households than before. The 2000 census in the US revealed that the nuclear family with two parents made up just 53 per cent of households, compared with 61 per cent in 1980 and 78 per cent in 1950. People living on their own without children reached 31 per cent of the population in the same period, up from 26 per cent in 1980 and 11 per cent half a century earlier.[6] A similar pattern is seen across the industrialized world. In some of the major cities, such as London and New York, people's social lives centre around the office, not the neighbourhood. If people have an empty apartment to return to at night, and don't know their neighbours, the importance of a vibrant social life at the office becomes central. If your office is an unfriendly, unmotivated place, they will move elsewhere, and there is no guarantee that it is only the less able who will move (if anything the more talented are more likely to be lured away by a competitor).

Population growth has not caught up with economic growth, and for as long as governments in richer countries remain wary of loosening immigration controls, skills shortages are likely to remain a recurring feature.

This is your workforce: skilled, stroppy, desperate for social contact in your workspace, and in increasingly short supply. Motivating them, giving them a reason for doing their best for you, is no longer an option. They are responsible for delivering the promises you have made to the chairman, or to the board, so how you handle them is a key part of your role – perhaps the most important part. It is not a peripheral, 'soft' matter.

This is your workforce: skilled, stroppy, desperate for social contact in your workspace, and in increasingly short supply.

That's the bad news. The good news is that the new breed are also technologically savvy, intellectually curious, and inventive. The profits of handling them astutely are handsome indeed.

George's story – a changing world

I never thought it would be like this … A rolling stone gathers no moss … well, is gathering moss a good thing?

When George graduated from high school with four A grades in his A-levels (the highest possible score in the UK schools examination system), it was clear to him and his family that he would go to Oxford, get a degree and work in the City. Both his dad and his cousin David had done the same. He planned to get a job in one of the top City banks and stay there for the whole of his working life. He believed his job would be interesting, and looked forward to the possibility of working abroad. He was assured by numerous implicit, and occasionally explicit, messages from his family that if he worked hard and became an executive, he would work for only one employer. The company would look after him.

His first job in the City was with *the* top investment bank and, as both he and others expected, George was promoted almost every two to three years. He was seen as a high potential manager, and at the age of 33 was head of the Hong Kong office. By now he had married and was a proud family man with three children. His wife, however, felt homesick for her family, and as their oldest child was beginning school, they decided that they would like to return to the UK.

Assured that there would be a job for him, George returned to Britain. He was first surprised, and then annoyed, when he began to hear messages from his superiors that there may not, after all, be a role for him, or at least not one that he may want. Nonetheless his immediate boss told him: 'Don't worry; the bank will take care of you.'

Three months after his return, George was still in charge of 'special projects' and he was beginning to feel anxious. In the three years he had been in Hong Kong his extraordinarily long hours at work and sleepless nights at home had meant that he had had very little contact with many of his senior colleagues in Europe. He found that there were many new faces and he felt left out of conversations. He was also hearing restructuring rumours, but ignored them, knowing he was not going to be affected.

Three weeks before his 35th birthday George was told he had one hour to pack his belongings and given a generous package with outplacement support. All the promises of 'we will look after you … trust me' were now worthless.

It was a struggle to accept that there were no more jobs for life. He lost his self-confidence and struggled to come to terms with what had happened to him. In addition, the advice he was receiving through outplacement didn't make much sense. He heard nonsense about networking, focusing on real achievements, and clarity about career. It seemed vague, almost meaningless. He had worked hard; he had exceptional ability. His employer had mishandled him and now the adviser it had appointed was putting the focus on *his* attitude, even though it had been faultless throughout his many years at the bank.

Now, at the age of 47, George still remembers those few months of disillusionment with some pain. He still can't understand what really happened to him, even though, viewed in retrospect, he coped remarkably well. It took him five months to find another job, and he stayed there for four years. When he was 39 he was headhunted to the CFO role in another bank. Initially, he felt twangs of loyalty to the institution and his bosses, but he realized that this was an opportunity that was too good to miss. 'And who knows,' he had thought to himself, 'they might not want me around in a year or two anyway …'

He is now the CEO of an international financial services institution, which is the fourth organization that he has worked for. He manages his own career with his coach as carefully as he manages the business and his team. He knows that he will probably work for at least one other organization before he retires formally at the age of 65.

Rather abruptly, George, like many others who began their careers in the 1980s and 1990s, learned the hard way that there were unlikely to be jobs for life. He coaches others to manage their own careers. He also knows that most of his colleagues and friends will work in at least three or four different organizations. Looking back at what has happened to him since that rude awakening, he acknowledges that the richness of his experience in a number of businesses has also made him a highly desirable CEO on the job circuit.

'It's tough being a female executive in a man's world'

Women at, or heading for, the top in business face all the challenges of men and more. It would take another book to explore these in full, and some have been written that explore women's role and contribution to management.[7] Here we focus on two aspects.

The first is the higher expectations women have of themselves (and that others sometimes have of women). Relinquishing the 'leader must not have faults' myth is a necessary step for all leaders, but for a woman – always fearing the snide comments that are likely to accompany any business failure with which she is associated – it is especially difficult. We will look further at the matter of exploring and understanding your weaknesses and strengths in Chapters 4 and 5, which concentrate on feedback from your team and self-awareness.

The second is the decision on starting a family, which necessarily has a bigger impact on women's career planning than on men's.

On the first of these, we record the views of Barbara Moorhouse, former finance director at IT firm Kewill Systems:

'When I began I felt that I had to be seen as superwoman. If you are female you feel you have less room for manoeuvre; that nothing can go wrong under your control. You start to try to become superhuman. There is a feeling that you are judged more harshly than men, and this results in you becoming more reserved.

'Earlier in my career I would only relax with people who knew me well. At a former company a colleague said to me: "Give people time to get to know you; don't be so super-efficient or concerned with being perfect; when people know you they really like you, and you are not just that woman who drives results." It is easier to be demonized as a woman.

'In my experience there are two camps of executive women. One group, particularly older ones, are prima donnas and although they complain about being victimized they get a kick out of being the only woman at the top and are hostile to other women. I have tried to work with women from this group and it is difficult.

'The second group likes to sponsor and support other women. I am delighted to see other women getting promoted because it is important. One of the nice things about the IT industry is that there are some senior women managers.'

She argues that it is important to challenge people from time to time on whether gender plays a part in decisions:

'We've had advisers pitching to us recently. Two of my team were finding it hard to rate highly two of the prospective candidates, who were women. I said to my colleagues (who are men): "Can I talk something through with you? It's occurred to me that both of the two representatives whom you rated lower are women. It could be that they are more junior than the male candidate, but could you please think about whether in your mind there is something about gender?" Neither of them is misogynist in any way, and they gave me a very reasoned view – but now at least I hope they would think about whether there is a gender issue.

'In this issue there is so much about female behaviour; fixing the women, or fixing the attitudes of very senior men. We need to fix the views of more junior men.'

This last point about attitudinal matters is particularly significant. It's easy to assume that, because of the emergence of high-profile business women such as Anita Roddick, Carly Fiorina and Marjorie Scardino, that the elevation to equality of opportunity and a gender-neutral workplace is both ineluctable and a short distance away. In fact, some research indicates that deeply rooted biases persist, are shifting slowly, and may even be in reverse in a few circumstances.[8]

For the foreseeable future, there are likely to be formidable extra pressures on ambitious women, simply because they are women.

This book primarily concerns developing the generic attributes of leadership that are constant across cultures and gender. The point here to note is that this personal development doesn't happen in isolation from matters such as demography, societal changes and gender. From an individual woman executive's point of view, there is still too much pressure on her to be seen to be better than the rest, and to have to consider such matters as maternity policies when choosing an employer. From an employer's point of view, the need to attract and retain the best women managers is actually increasing, so business sense ought to point in the same direction as political correctness.

We hope you don't feel daunted by this list of challenges. There is no need to be: if you are already in a senior post you will be familiar with them, and if not it is better to be prepared. Of all the challenges, perhaps the one that is commonest is the matter of feeling alone, and we hope that this chapter will have illustrated that this feeling, and attendant anxieties over being 'good enough', is common to all business leaders, including the most successful ones. The point is not to deny any feeling of loneliness or inadequacy, but to experience it, acknowledge it and learn. It makes the achievements you realize even more rewarding.

The point is not to deny any feeling of loneliness or inadequacy, but to experience it, acknowledge it and learn.

PERSONAL REVIEW QUESTIONNAIRE

These questions will help you gain a sense of where you are, help you identify your degree of support or isolation, and indicate some developmental priorities.

Network support

Comment on the support of friends and soulmates you have at work.

1 How many people are there at work whom you trust, to whom you can really talk about how you feel?
2 When you leave the office, do you have friends and/or family who really understand your passions, fears and anxieties?
3 Do you have a strong support system at home where you feel relaxed and can wind down?

Preparing for the role after next

It's important to bear in mind how you are preparing not only for your next role, but also the role after next.

4 Do you have (or are you planning to acquire) international experience?
5 Have you thought about how you might work on a project which is outside your direct remit?
6 Are you (or are you planning to be) a non-executive/ independent director?
7 Are you clear about what makes a successful leader? How would you evaluate yourself against these leadership behaviours and skills?

For women

8 Are you the only woman on the board or on the management team?

9 Are you aware of how you might feel more comfortable in some of the male-orientated activities (for example, in outward-bound courses) or evening meetings?

Impact on the team

10 How do you think your PA would describe you?

11 Do people often interrupt you when you are in your office or workspace, or do you look unapproachable? (Check to see if physically you are easily approachable, or for example, if there are bookcases, walls or secretaries blocking the entrance to your office.)

12 Do you smile when people meet you in the corridor?

13 Would you say people feel really nervous about phoning you or sending you an e-mail?

14 Do people often ask you to join them for lunch or even a sandwich lunch?

chapter two
your behaviour is worth money – the links between what you do and how the business is

Learning points from this chapter

- The performance of your people is a strategic matter.

- Investors are starting to ask about leadership capability and succession planning.

- Emotional intelligence is the natural partner to rational analysis.

- Industry and technical knowledge combined with a strong leadership style make the complete leader.

- 'If your head goes down, the business will follow.'

- There is no point in thinking 'if only'; we are not victims of fate.

- We can always improve.

- We learn from what we do well.

- Improvement is the opposite of ditching your personality.

Behaviour and leadership style: does it make a difference?

For some managers, it is conceptually difficult to accept that changing something as personal as their behaviour can have benefits that are measurable on the bottom line of a corporation.

The links are easier to understand if we remind ourselves that sales, revenue and profits are simply the end result of what people do. Profits come from customers, by way of staff, and financial results are simply the effects of these interactions. Seen in this light, the performance of people becomes strategic, and not a supplementary matter.

Profits come from customers, by way of staff, and financial results are simply the effects of these interactions.

Consider the following observation by Gerry Robinson, former chief executive of Granada:

'It is always people. Always. You know, the number of times that you are told that something is impossible and can't be done and then someone else comes along and says, "No, we can do it!" And they do it. It really is always about getting the right person in the right role.

'Most people are better than you think, but really really good people whom you can absolutely trust are very difficult to come by. You should make sure that you reward them, that they have a career path. You should look after them and cherish them because they are a rarity.

'Management quality is underestimated. You tend to get an approach to business which is analytical about questions like, "What is its place in the market?" "How big is the market?" "What is the share?" "Who are the competitors?" All of which is important, but almost never do you have the question: "Well, hang on, who is actually managing this? How smart are they? How lucky have they been?" It is underestimated – probably less than it used to be, as there is a greater sense now that if you get the right person then things can happen.'

The quality of people in the management team matters, as Gerry Robinson emphasizes; the quality of the staff as a whole matters; and the motivation of the staff depends on management. Staff pick up their clues from you, the leader. Later in this chapter we will come across an executive, Ian Carlisle of the British company Autoglass, whose behaviour played a part in turning the business round. Behaviour can be worth millions of pounds, dollars or euros to your company. It is not fiscally neutral.

Management is sometimes not really seen as a human skill, by its practitioners or by some cynical detractors. It is somehow 'up there', inhabiting the space of strategic vision or jargon-filled nonsense, depending on your prejudice. Both these views are inaccurate and the latter is demeaning. It's more accurate to see leadership as a complex skill like Java programming or playing the violin. It is also valid to recognize our importance as leaders and senior managers, as the people who, through our logistical, analytical and motivational abilities, run the organizations that deliver goods, services and entertainments to people and make civilization possible. It's easy to demean ourselves, or be affected by insults like 'fat cats', and to forget the importance of our role and also of the importance of developing our skills.

Companies may think: 'We've thrived for 150 years without fussing about leadership development and we had record results this year.' What one often finds, however, is that the old family members of a private firm, for example, may be experienced, dedicated trainers who engage in induction and development programmes for future leaders without calling it 'training' or 'development'. They instinctively know that this is actually important for success. They have known about emotional intelligence for decades, but instinctively, and unspoken. Because it's behind the scenes, not the subject of press releases, and long-term, the links between this activity and business success are not always evident externally.

In any event executives increasingly can't ignore managerial development – including the subtler skills of behaviour, motivation and handling relationships – even if they are inclined to. Not only are more individual managers recognizing the importance of managerial abilities and the connection with bottom-line performance, but there are also external pressures. Investors are unhappy with the speculation that often accompanies annual reports and the chairman's statements, and are inadequately informed by the accounts (which, after Enron, we now know can bear little relation to reality). Investors need to form some sense of a company's potential, and hence its value. They are asking – sometimes directly, sometimes indirectly – about managerial ability. They are putting a price on your ability to lead and handle people.

In a recent newspaper article, Warburg Dillon Read stated, 'the value of £500m on Granada management is based on analysis of earnings growth compared with peers.' This may seem a crude measure, but the importance is in the focus: Warburg Dillon Read are asking about managerial ability. The establishment of a sound strategy and a coherent business structure is not enough. What analysts and investors are also examining is whether there is a process in place to implement a solid foundation of appropriate skills and behaviours. In other words, is this precious managerial ability due solely to a talented individual or two currently on board, or is there also a programme of development and succession planning that will maximize the chance of developing and attracting high performers in the future?

Can I change? Will it change my personality?

Once you accept intellectually the need for development of management skills and behaviours, there can still remain doubts about your ability to adapt. We can believe, falsely, that we 'can't change' if we are from a particular profession, or we are over 40, or if we are married, or some other reason. This chapter explores the fears and doubts that inhibit us, and encourages a belief in relentless improvement. Let's take some of the fears or grounds for scepticism in turn.

'Emotional, behavioural stuff is just trendy Californian thinking'

An understandable fear is that talk of behaviour, or emotional intelligence, is 'new age' trendy thinking, and that being an executive means being rational, analytical and decisive. We argue that this is not an 'either/or' situation. Analysis and rational thought remain as important as ever for business leadership. What we seek to illustrate through this book is that leadership behaviour is the manner in which rational decisions are put into practice, and to show you how this is done. Your people are more likely to achieve your vision – or a shared vision – if they understand what the vision and the strategy are, and are enthused to deliver it. They may achieve even more than you hope if they are truly motivated. You may learn from an intelligent, dynamic team. This is not a weakness in you, but quite the opposite; it is part of the virtuous circle in which leader and team are growing and delivering exceptional performance together.

Once you accept intellectually the need for development of management skills and behaviours, there can still remain doubts about your ability to adapt.

Sue Turner, human resources director at the IT and Operations Shared Service Organization at Barclays Bank, comments on the experience of members of an executive team that she has helped coach and put together:

'Before, they would have been sceptical about "pink and fluffy" team-building; but now they are up for it.'

We'll return to the experience of this Barclays executive team in Chapter 4.

There is an increasing amount of research indicating that rational and emotional thought are not really separate. We engage intellectually with the ideas that please us most. Activity in the parts of the brain that are most closely identified with reason occurs in conjunction with similar activity in the emotional department of the cerebrum.[9] This would indicate that it is a mistake to suppose that we can divorce analysis and strategy-setting from behaviour and feelings.

Some of the most recent research on human expertise actually inverts some common assumptions. It asserts that where rational thought is dominant, one achieves only a moderate level of competence, and that for the highest levels of expertise you need to bring in intuition and subconscious learning.[10] The concert pianist is not thinking, 'four demi-semi-quavers followed by a quaver;' he or she is in such complete mastery of the pattern and mood of the piece that they've moved far beyond thinking in such linear, rational steps. In the same way the complete leader moves effortlessly between the six leadership styles that we set out, deploying each one as the occasion demands, and is accomplished in emotionally intelligent ways of behaving. Each of the styles incorporates both rational and emotional strands. Deciding to deploy your emotional intelligence is a rational course of action.

In the words of Andy Logan, director of the Centaur Leadership Programme at Cranfield University in the UK:

'Rational frameworks are practical necessities for those who would lead; but it is imagination and heart that inspires others to follow.'

In a significant way, the importance of a leader's behaviour actually increases as he or she becomes more senior. Even in informal, low-hierarchy workplaces, the comments and behaviour of the leader are picked up or observed minutely by the team surrounding him or her. This happens consciously and subconsciously.

The conscious clues come mostly from language. The comments of a senior executive, whether made in a formal setting or as an aside, are carefully noted by others in the team and organization, and may form the focus of gossip. If anything, the informal comments create more fascination, as they are often taken to be a clue to the 'real' thinking that lies behind the official statements. Greg Lewin, president Shell Global Solutions, comments:

'What was a surprise (as I reached a senior position) was the powerful impact that your behaviour can have. When you are cast as a decision-maker or first among equals or leader, your behaviour has much more impact than previously. So it wasn't a surprise that my behaviour had an impact; what was a surprise was the extent to which this was so. To you, what could be throw-away lines could be treated with extreme significance by other people.

'In one case I could have been much more coaching than challenging (in dealing with a performance issue). I had underestimated the fact that my opinion was so valuable to him. He was going to take heed, so I didn't have to put it in an emphatic way.'

Subconsciously, behaviour infuses the surrounding environment. An irritable, stressed leader creates an irritable, stressed organization. A high-energy, innovative leader tends to create empowered, creative teams. We'll discuss this further in Chapter 5 under 'Feelings are contagious' (page 103).

'Knowledge of the industry is more important than leadership style'

As with our comments on rationality and emotion, this again is not an 'either/or'. An organization needs strong specialist knowledge and abilities as well as mature leadership style. It is, however, a fair criticism of management training in the past that too much emphasis has been placed on generic skills and arguably not enough on the specialist needs of the fashion business/nuclear industry/public transport or whatever specialist area you are in. This objection is therefore perfectly understandable.

We would make two points: firstly, this book makes a working assumption that in your organization you have the requisite technical skills both individually and collectively. Secondly – and more importantly – because the transformation of becoming a complete leader means empowering and understanding each other more fully, we can actually better understand the technical skills and deficiencies that the organization has through the development that we set out in this book. If, for example, an individual feels cowed by a bullying boss, or unrecognized by a leader who can't listen, then that individual's knowledge of an area of the business, say, or good relationships with certain suppliers, or marketing qualification, will go ignored and unused. Complete leaders, by incorporating coaching and democratic styles as well as those of direction and authority, can learn more about the skills of a team and deploy them on the organization's behalf.

Criticisms of genericism in the past are understandable, but we are talking about a rather different approach to management here. In the traditional MBA, for example, there has been much emphasis on strategic analysis and financial control; treating any organization as being mechanical and much like any other, in the hope that generic analytical approaches could work in any situation. This is not the same as the combination of a range of managerial styles and emotionally mature interpersonal skills that we set out in this book. It is the combination of these complete leadership skills with the technical, customer and industry-related ability that a business needs.

Ian Carlisle's story – How a company was transformed

'If your head goes down, the business will follow.'

A perfect illustration of this combination of industry knowledge and personal skills comes in the story of Ian Carlisle, managing director of UK firm Autoglass, the leading windscreen provider for the UK motorist. He was elevated to the post of MD, having been groomed by the former MD – though the promotion came a little early for Ian, he felt, as he had been operations director for only 18 months when the move was first put to him.

As he assumed the new role, a new logistics and computer system came on line and implemented a 'big bang' that had significant performance issues. It led to serious problems with suppliers, increasing debt and weakening morale among staff. Ian, who had had a coach for three years, used the support that she had to offer. Most of the solutions were of a technical and industry-specific nature, and Ian drew heavily on his own knowledge of the business's systems to map out solutions, but coaching – and the strengthening of Ian's personal skills – played a role in the turnaround that was achieved. Judge for yourself how important each strand was as Ian relates the story.

'When I took over as managing director [moving up from the post of operations director], the company had just implemented the new system. It had gone badly wrong. After all this great preparation for the leadership role I had hit the ground and the business was facing its biggest challenge in years. The performance with the new system was slow; it just didn't work at a sufficient speed to cope with the demand and the business fell behind. Debts went up. Cash flow struggled and our service standards slipped. It was my first month, November 1999, and I was in at the deep end.

'What I thought was going to happen didn't. I thought the business was on an even keel. Business got behind and motivation among staff fell dramatically. Customer perceptions were poor, because we were letting motorists down, and the big accounts were run on the basis of efficiency and we were not efficient. I had more problems than I had ever experienced in my career within two months of my promotion.

'It was always "going to get better," . . . but it didn't. Or people would say, "we'll tweak it," but they were being over-optimistic. We had all invested so much in it that we felt it should work, and that it must work; but it didn't. So, in terms of my work with my coach, it was how to energize the business as this was not going to be a quick fix. In truth, there was no magic formula. My coach gave me advice about my demeanour and confidence. The best advice was when she said: "If your head goes down then the business will follow. You have to stay positive and show tenacity – the leader has a major impact on the business climate."

'You have to err on the positive side on balance; it is a case of mapping a way out, and I was doing that taking a very complex problem and devising a planned series of critical paths, and mobilizing resources. We had to invest even more, at a time when the company was slipping. The normal reaction when a company is underperforming is that you don't spend, but that would have exacerbated the problem. So we had to invest significantly and hire more people. Sometimes leading is having the strength to go against the norm and take a long-term view.

'There were difficult meetings towards the end of the year. We finished 1999 with bad results for the year. My honest feeling at the time was one of total isolation, irrespective of the fact that I had a coach, and I had a boss [the group CEO] who knows a lot about the business. It was hard, because every day above and below me people were looking to me to get us out of the situation. I knew that shareholders were beginning to worry, as the biggest business in the group was underperforming significantly. I knew that people within the business were feeling frustrated; like they were wading through treacle. I have to say that those are moments when, no matter how much personal confidence you have, you feel very isolated at the top.

In resolving business performance issues that are complex like that one, these are areas where coaching is limited.

'It was an area where I needed industry-specific skills. We needed more hardware; extra disk space and to get through the backlog; we threw people at it. We just had to. The route became both a technical solution and pure tenacity – it is amazing how the business responds if the leader is outwardly confident and invests real time in taking the team with you.

'Towards the end of the hard period, feeling isolated, I thought very clearly that if I didn't improve then it was all on my head. That was the time when I needed the coach. I felt unfairly treated. I took on the responsibility at a time that wasn't right. I was given a clear indication that unless I got out of it it was on my head. I felt a lot of resentment. My coach helped me manage that resentment. She said, "It's the way of the world." It made me mature in the responsibilities of being the leader. She said, "It's not fair; but it's yours to sort out or leave." She was most directive. At a time that I wanted some tender loving care she gave me a kick up the backside. She said, "Your boss is an executive and is a major shareholder; and his shareholders are on his back. It is tough, but make your choices work for you."

'Since 2000 we have started to pull away significantly. By the end of 2000 we had grown by 40 per cent, and in 2001 we grew by a further 25 per cent in a market with declining margins. We took £15m of costs out. I learned more in nine months than I probably would have learned in five years as managing director in easier times. Once I was out of the difficult period I could become strategic and forward-looking. I attacked the business issues/opportunities much more quickly than would have been the case. I had gained a level of confidence by knowing that if I could turn things around from those complex problems then anything else in business is just a matter of prioritizing.

'By mid-2000 we had a new business structure. We took layers of management out, streamlined operational efficiency, and improved service to the customer. We took debt down by 40 per cent in the year. Market share improved by 4 percentage points, despite the fact that the RAC [a major national breakdown service provider] entered the market, and so did Ford via its Kwik-Fit acquisition. In 2001 we recorded our highest staff satisfaction result in the history of Autoglass.

'Once I had the business moving again, I didn't see as much of my coach. I felt that all I needed was a phone call every three months. Coaching is about being honest with yourself and your coach. Using the expert mechanisms that she can provide to understand your strengths and weaknesses. If you are not honest you will never get anything out of it.'

We return to the subject of coaching in Chapter 6.

'If only . . .' and 'I should . . .'

It is well established in psychological study that humans display a capacity for irrational beliefs that can hold us back; beliefs that often take the form of internal voices instructing us. We can re-indoctrinate ourselves as adults with these, according to Windy Dryden, professor of counselling at Goldsmiths College London. She says:

'Irrational beliefs are evaluations of personal significance stated in absolute terms such as 'must', 'should', 'ought' and 'have to'. They are rigid, illogical, inconsistent with reality and self- and other-defeating. It is noted that people often change their desires into demands.'[11]

As well as the 'shoulds' in our minds, we often have 'if onlys' which similarly reflect our beliefs about the ingredients for success, but are disabling because we are putting our faith in luck. Some examples of those that are common in executives include:

- ◆ 'If only I'd gone to Yale/Cambridge.'

- ◆ 'If only I'd been born with charisma.'

- ◆ 'Why should I change? I've done well enough up until now.'

- ◆ 'I can't change now I'm over 40.'

Ever thought one of those? It would be surprising if you haven't. They are typical of the myths that can arise with surprising, unspoken force in our society. Whether they come from the Protestant work ethic, the Cold War, or our grandparents' experience in the Great Depression is a matter for enquiry that would take us beyond the limits of this practical book. The point is to acknowledge them; to recognize that they are not all negative – generally they tell us that it is good to achieve and to have ambitions – but to recognize also that they can hold us back.

Let's take each one in turn.

'If only I'd gone to Yale/Cambridge.'

In a recent article, the management thinker Henry Mintzberg identified the most admired chief executives of recent corporate history in North America. The shortlist was perfectly predictable: Jack Welch, Andy Grove, Bill Gates and Bob Galvin. Then he made a comment about their qualifications. None of them had an MBA, and two of them had actually dropped out of college.

The human brain is the most advanced, versatile, adaptable and improvable entity in the biological world. It can recover from poor schooling, from bullying, even from substance abuse. But it thrives on continual exercise, a good diet, stimulus and challenge. We accept the need to go to the gym to exercise our bodies, but can sometimes neglect our minds. When did we last do mental arithmetic, learn a foreign language or read *New Scientist*? Anyone can become smarter than they currently are, and the truth is that we don't know just how smart we can become. That is a tremendously exciting thought.

Anyone can become smarter than they currently are, and the truth is that we don't know just how smart we can become.

Those who passed a difficult entrance examination at age 18 for a prestigious university are doubtless well endowed with the grey matter, but they could be letting it go stale through failing to set themselves enough challenges, or through drinking too much, for example.

Once we enter the corporate world we tend to be on more or less the same playing field. If you are in a senior position, the likelihood is that you deserve to be there. You have the abilities.

'If only I'd been born with charisma.'

This is one of the most dangerous tripwires for the potentially complete leader. We all know someone who was surrounded by acolytes from a young age, who just had to hint that he or she wanted a party and their house was full, who attract people by their charm to work for them. They seem to lead quite naturally, and can be successful (though intriguingly, not always). Especially when we

are young, such individuals can provoke powerful feelings of
inadequacy when we compare ourselves with them.

Charisma simply means the ability to attract people and their
attention. Research on leadership does not identify this as a key
attribute in itself, although it can strengthen the authoritative style
(see page 47). Magnetic personalities may have many attributes, but
they may lack some too. When the business writer Jim Collins
researched the best performing US companies in the past 30 years
he listed 11 companies which had outperformed GE over that time.
All of them had rather unsexy images, and all were headed by
'anonymous insiders'.[12] True leadership comes from a rich blend of
attributes, and the ability to draw a crowd is not the most important.
One attribute of some charismatic individuals is the ability to create
a good press, which says little about a person's ability to lead an
organization. Not only is it of limited use to the company, it can
tempt the individual to neglect his or her personal development in
more important leadership qualities.

The unique gift of people with great charisma is to attract people and
enthuse them to work towards a goal. This is only useful if it is
unaccompanied by bullying, and if the goal makes sense for all the
people involved. Complete leadership involves a much wider range
of abilities, as we'll see throughout this book.

'Why should I change? I've done well enough up until now.'

'I can't change now I'm over 40.'

There is a strong belief in many of us that we can't change what we
are and how we behave. Change is often not even a considered
option. This belief is deep-rooted, and even more so if you have been
successful. The natural rhetorical question that arises in our minds is,
'Why should I change what I'm doing when I've done well enough
up until now?'

There are problems with this attitude, however. Firstly, it is simply
not true that we can't change: how did we manage to move beyond

high-school levels of ability and self-awareness without changing? Secondly, moving to an executive post introduces formidable new challenges which are met by developing both analytical and interpersonal skills, as the case studies throughout this book illustrate. Thirdly, even if we have strong powers as a top executive, and a track record of success: why put a cap on further ambitions by pretending there is no scope for improvement?

The key question to ask yourself is: 'Are there some habits or behaviours that, if I were to do more or less of them, would enable me to be even more successful?' For example, if you raised your self-awareness, and understood the impact you had on others, you could then decide which behaviours or habits you might wish to change.

Why then – even after you have made a decision about something about yourself that you would like to change and you know it would be really valuable to you if you did change it – is it so hard to make those changes? We'll discuss this matter more in Chapter 6, but for now it is illustrative to reflect on both the possibility and the difficulties of personal change and development.

For example, Gillian, the regional head of a large manufacturing business who was based in Peru, had participated in 360-degree appraisal every year for five years. The feedback was consistently the same. She was seen as charismatic, energetic, decisive and visionary. But there were also comments every year that she did not listen. Why was it only now that she had decided that she needed coaching to help her to learn how to listen? Why had she not bothered to do anything about it for the five years previously? She is highly intelligent, and knew that such development was key to her future success. In Gillian's case, the possibility of moving into the chief operating officer role made her sit up and realize that she might not get it if she did not change.

So, is change only possible if we receive awkward feedback, or if we miss the promotion we wanted, or if we are made redundant? Is it possible to want to change and strengthen our emotional competencies even if we are doing really well and are seen as highly successful?

Is change only possible if we receive awkward feedback, or if we miss the promotion we wanted, or if we are made redundant?

We believe that it is, and this leads us on to what we believe is an important principle.

We learn from what we do well, not from our mistakes

There is a Gary Larson 'Far Side' cartoon where a mother from the Classical World is complaining to her teenage son: 'And another thing, I want you to be more assertive. I'm tired of everyone calling you "Alexander the Pretty-Good".'

One intriguing new academic theory is that we tend to move towards the image we project for our future. Call ourselves 'great', and we are more likely to become great. One note of caution, however: this is a developmental process, not a magic solution. The theory, known as 'Appreciative inquiry', was developed by Dr David Cooperrider at the Case Western Reserve University in the early 1990s. He argues that we tend to move in the direction of the subject matter of our conversations, and the content of our dreams. If we talk about problems, we inhabit problems. If we talk about achievements, we achieve. There is a 'Pygmalion effect' that has been observed in education: if teachers are told that their pupils are bright they are more likely to be effective teachers.[13]

The theory rests on an observation that the human brain does not obey the instruction 'don't' very well. It is a common experience of many people who have played sport. If the coach says, 'Don't go into the rough,' or, 'Don't serve into the net,' then sure enough we do. If we focus on the positive goal, we are more likely to achieve it.

Appreciative inquiry, when applied in organizations, involves the use of small and large group meetings to begin a process of sharing ideas on what is working well, using this to set a vision, and then working towards that vision. One academic article describes the process as follows:

'Consider two ways you as a manager might welcome new employees. If you ask them to tell you about problems they encounter as they get acquainted with their new colleagues and new job, then you are, no matter how well intended, planting seeds of problems and you will most certainly hear about them. If, on the other hand, you request that they try to discover what contributes to their new work group's high levels of cooperation and success, you are planting seeds of learning about cooperation and success.'[14]

This is obviously applicable to individuals as well. As humans we are prone to creating self-fulfilling prophesies, so it is better to make sure that our prophesies are positive.

Claire Hall-Moore, associate partner at consultancy group Accenture, comments:

'I really wanted to get promoted to the role of Associate Partner. Working with my coach [Susan Bloch], I realized that an important step in career development is to perceive yourself in the position and the role. If you start to perceive yourself as being able to do things, you behave in a commensurate manner and that also starts to impact on the people around you. For me, it was a really good piece of advice, and coaching helped me to be able to perceive myself as part of the leadership team already [before promotion], and to behave in that way. I think it worked very well and it helped me make the transition into my new role.'

In this book we invite you to build on your strengths as well as acknowledge areas for development. Logically, there ought to be more to learn from strengths than from weaknesses. If we are doing something poorly, there is an infinite number of options for change, and simply being reminded of this offers no clues for improvement.

If we are doing something right, however, we already have access to the secrets for further development. Thinking about our strengths has the added advantage of boosting our confidence, which increases our workrate and motivation – and our ability to address weaknesses.

If we are doing something poorly, there is an infinite number of options for change, and simply being reminded of this offers no clues for improvement.

It is difficult, however, either to develop strengths or to attend to weaknesses if we do not know what they are. Commonly, executives have an inaccurate perception of themselves simply because they have rarely asked anyone for feedback. This is why in this book we will put so much emphasis on developing self-awareness, and creating a personal scorecard for yourself. This will serve as a benchmark against which to mark your progress.

Do I have to change my personality?

This combination of self-awareness, improving strengths and identifying weaknesses implies a focus on the person you already are. It means tapping into latent abilities that you hold. It's the opposite of ditching or changing your personality; it is allowing all of your abilities to shine, including those which have been so hidden that you didn't realize you had them.

We define six core qualities which, if combined effectively, create complete leadership. Our starting point is this: you already demonstrate the six styles. You already excel in some of them. You possess an infinite capacity to develop and learn when to use each one. Our purpose is to unlock the genius in you, not convert you into 'Management Prototype X'. Our categorization of six managerial styles gives us a vocabulary to talk about the abilities that create good leadership, not to force you into a box against your will.

This book is based on research, not good intentions. Remember the study from Chapter 1? The climate of the organization – whether or not people feel a positive buzz about the place – has a tremendous bearing on results.

The research informs the process as well as describing the results. The steps we outline in the following chapters are based on decades of work with senior executives in real business situations, and on monitoring and measuring the results. Leadership is learnable and measurable, and it makes a dramatic impact on the bottom line. Let's begin the analysis that will prepare you for improvement.

chapter three

take a picture of yourself
– learn about the type of
leader you already are

Learning points from this chapter

◆ We exhibit leadership styles whether we realize this or not; there is no such thing as 'neutral' or emotion-free leadership.

◆ Leadership can be usefully categorized into six styles: authoritativeness and coaching are the most effective in the long term, but an ability to display all is best.

◆ Measuring the organizational climate gives a key indicator, predictive of financial success.

◆ Chief executives, even the best ones, often have poor awareness of their most important abilities.

◆ The key leadership styles are most effective when combined with high levels of emotional intelligence.

In this chapter we will learn of the importance of gaining a rounded view on how you come across to others, most especially those who work closest with you. You may already have been through 360-degree appraisals, and you may have a fair idea of others' perceptions of your strengths and weaknesses. The aim here is to reproduce, and probably add to, that feedback in a way that can be plotted on a chart and used to measure progress. It may sound formulaic, but the picture it produces is unique to you and has been proven to be effective in the development of leadership skills. By keeping the measures consistent you can ensure that improvement is always being monitored against the same benchmark.

One point to emphasize is that we exhibit some or all of these styles *whether we recognize this or not*. This will become evident as you begin the self-assessment and gather the feedback from your direct reports. There is no such thing as neutral, or emotion-free, leadership. Every interaction we have with our boss or our direct reports constitutes a form of relationship, and the more impersonal or 'rational' approaches will show up somewhere on the grid that we set out.

We'll map your perception of yourself, and those of others working with you, against six key leadership styles. But before describing the process, here's a description of the styles.

The six leadership styles

Authoritative leadership

Authoritative leadership means giving a real sense of direction that is ambitious, but realistic. It means having a vision, without lapsing into fantasy. It gives strong direction, but unlike the coercive style, implicitly acknowledges that employees' commitment must be earned. A coercive leader says, 'Go there!' An authoritative leader says, 'Come with me'. At the very beginning of the book, we noted a psychological experiment showing how someone in authority can have great power over individuals. But the experiment in question involved an authority figure crossing the road despite the 'WAIT' sign. Had he or she stayed on the kerb while ordering others to cross, the result would have been very different.

An authoritative leader never loses sight of the core purpose of the business and understands that this overriding sense of purpose is also the matter that most motivates employees. He or she can easily rise above internal politics, bureaucracy and jargon to see things from a customer's perspective and remind people within the organization what they are there for.

An authoritative leader never loses sight of the core purpose of the business.

People want leadership from their leaders. This obvious statement merits inclusion because sometimes we can be lulled into thinking that because we are heading a firm of highly intelligent software developers, say, or a team of able executives, we can let these high-performing people sort things out for themselves. This is not so. A leader sets the vision, defines the culture, and sets norms and values for the group or organization. He or she encourages and coaches people, but will discipline them if they have broken these agreed norms and conventions. One recent study concluded: 'Our research showed that on outstanding teams the leader gave far clearer direction than on average or poor-performing teams . . . When the team leader does not provide it [direction], a leadership vacuum is created, one that all members rush to fill with their own individual priorities and goals.'

It added: 'As CEO you should never assume that because your top team includes bright, successful individuals, there is no need to establish clear norms. Our research suggests the opposite is true: because top teams are composed of such strong personalities, clear norms are even more important.'[15]

If you are feeling unsure about the direction, but sense that the staff need reassurance, it's best to map out a vision, and the route to that goal with the risks involved. The alternative, extreme approaches that are often taken – to no good effect – are either to pretend there are no problems or to convey your own anxieties.

Some executives have developed the authoritative style through training on how to give public speeches or deal with the media. They conceive of themselves as presenting, or being 'on stage' all the time in management. But this does *not* mean being fake! In the words of Barbara Moorhouse, former finance director of IT firm Kewill Systems:

'Although I think of it as a stage I am not acting. You have to have integrity. You are being yourself but it is that part of yourself that the company needs at that time.'

(See page 154 for more.)

In a few, rare, occasions the authoritative style is not appropriate. This is where the goal is already well established and an experienced team is co-operating effectively towards that end. Here the leader is better employed adopting the affiliative or democratic styles (see below).

Coaching

After the authoritative style, the coaching style is the next most effective in the long term, Hay research has shown. The complete leader can deploy all six styles, but if you only have two, it's better to have these two.

Coaching is the ability to bring the best out in others. If an analogy with a team game is taken, the basketball player who is brilliant but never passes to a team mate is going to be much less successful than one who brings others into play. Mature leaders who are comfortable with the coaching role will take as much pleasure from a protégé completing a project or clinching a deal as they would if they had carried out the task themselves.

The key to unlocking the coach and mentor in you – that to an extent is shared with the democratic style (see below) – concerns abandoning fear. Too often we suppress a subordinate's or a colleague's endeavour in one area because we perceive it as a threat to us. There is an internal voice that tells us, 'I mustn't let Gill head a project because I have project management skills and people may think she is better than me; I want to be the only one in the team to be seen to have those skills.' Put in such bald terms, it is easy to see that this reaction is based on a fear of inadequacy, and insecurity. It is an irrational instinct that is holding back the development of Gill, of the organization and of yourself (because you could learn from her, and gain the credit for bringing the best out of her). Chances to win orders are being squandered, and the probability of losing skills to a competitor is increased, if she is thwarted in her ambition to develop.

The problem is that you may appear to be decisive and authoritative, at least superficially, if you squash a subordinate's aspiration to develop. It appears that you are increasing or at least consolidating your influence. This is an illusion, because your staff are volunteers, and their motivation and contribution have a major impact on the ability of the team to deliver the strategic objectives that you have promised to the board. So you have increased your influence relative to the individual you have put down, but decreased it in the wider world, and diminished your chances of pleasing the shareholders, except in the rare cases where a coercive style is appropriate (see below). These are heavily circumscribed, as we will explain.

The complete leader is accomplished in the coaching style. We deliberately begin with the authoritative and coaching styles because research indicates them to be the most effective. There is a powerful underlying message in the coaching style which says to staff: 'I want you to succeed.' By contrast the bully says, 'I want to find you out.' For an example of the coaching style, see the case study of Dave Bennett (page 60).

Democratic leadership

A leader in democratic mode asks the staff or the team: 'What shall we do? You decide.' Put simply in this way, it looks like an abdication of responsibility by the leader and can indeed be viewed that way on occasion by the staff, who reason, 'So-and-So is paid all that money to make the difficult decisions, so why should we have to?' The pure democratic style is only useful every now and then, but a dose of it incorporated with other styles can be tremendously effective. Note how, in Dave Bennett's story, it was the suggestion of a junior member of staff which, once acted on by the team, led to the business taking off. This is where the democratic style can really score.

Democracy works well when employees are already highly motivated, the goals are clear, but there is a need to elicit ideas from the team as to how to achieve those objectives. In practice, of course, the buck still lies with the leader, and use of the democratic style can be more akin to consultation than truly joint decision-making. This can sound confused and impractical: after all, if the leader makes the decision after all, was the consultation process cosmetic? And if the leader doesn't, is he or she really needed? The nature and usefulness of the process, however, depend on the relationships involved. In high-trust environments, genuine consensus can be reached and the beauty of this is that everyone is tied to the vision and has a sense of ownership. In other cases, staff respect the leader and recognize that their ideas have genuinely influenced strategy but that the decisions properly stay the responsibility of the leader; this latter case is more a combination of authoritativeness and democracy.

The most effective part of the democratic style is the empowerment and motivation people gain from having information shared. They can understand better the need for difficult decisions, for example, if they realize just how tough trading conditions are or how much raw material costs have risen.

The most effective part of the democratic style is the empowerment and motivation people gain from having information shared.

The pitfalls are that decision-making can be too slow. Democratic styles can be the result of indecisive leaders simply delaying difficult decisions, which often results in the cutbacks or other unpleasant outcomes being worse as well as later, than they would have been with more decisive action. The democratic style is one to avoid during a crisis.

Even in more benign circumstances, there can be much time wasted in meetings searching for an elusive consensus when achieving such unanimity was never likely.

The democratic style is not as positive on organizational climate as the authoritative or coaching styles.

Affiliative leadership

An affiliative leader prizes harmony and good relationships above all else. He or she goes to great lengths to ensure that people relate well together and that strong bonds between leader and team members, and among the team, are established. They will frequently treat the team to a meal out; they will celebrate successes openly; they will make sure no one is left out and that no resentment or injustice is allowed to fester.

Affiliative leaders give positive feedback continually, which is something that staff in most workplaces are starved of, and this has a powerful impact on performance.

Communication and trust are high priorities, and this can have a tremendously positive effect on teamwork. The exchange of ideas, security and familiarity that this engenders can aid innovation. It is notable that many entrepreneurial companies try to foster an affiliative ethos with casual dress and non-hierarchical leadership styles.

An affiliative style can engender formidable bonds of loyalty and commitment. People give of themselves above and beyond the call of duty, because they feel a strong emotional attachment to those they are working for.

In a similar way to the democratic mode, people feel a sense of ownership of the organization and that they have a stake in its future. The combination of these intangible assets with strong teamwork is something that can't simply be copied by a competitor. The affiliative style can be particularly effective in restoring teamwork where it has been badly damaged by excessive coercion in the recent past.[16]

Problems with the affiliative style are fairly obvious. As with the democratic style, important decisions can be left unmade while participation is prioritized. The emphasis on praise and harmony can lead to poor or lazy performance going unchallenged which, paradoxically, can actually poison working relationships. If, for example, an individual is often feigning illness or leaving early, with the result that the rest of the team are staying late to cover for him or her, the line manager is damaging workplace relationships as well as performance by neglecting to discipline the errant individual.

The affiliative style can be used effectively in combination with the authoritative style. This may sound like a marriage of opposites, but with the authoritative style, remember, you are setting goals and a vision, but leaving individuals and teams considerable autonomy in determining means to those ends.

Pace-setting

The pace-setting style is often dominant in an individual who is a technical expert, perhaps rather introverted, and is promoted to project leader or head of department with insufficient development of leadership skills.

The pace-setter says: 'Do it like me.' They carry out too many tasks themselves, either because they are more comfortable with technical tasks than in the leadership role or because they don't trust others to get it right – or a combination of the two. They are often unintentionally coercive, believing that it would be patronizing to coach or give direction to people. Their reluctance to delegate, however, can be demotivating for their direct reports as they have insufficient autonomy and diminished opportunity to hone their skills.

There are occasions, however, when pace-setting is valuable. Pace-setters do at least demand high standards and, as individuals who generally work to these high standards themselves, they can never be accused of being individuals who can 'teach but not do'. Where highly talented but lazy individuals need a strong role model, the pace-setter can provide one. The degree of interpersonal rivalry that the pace-setter unintentionally introduces can lead to high performance, provided the team has the requisite skills and a clear goal, meaning that the authoritative and coaching needs are *de facto* catered for.

The big weakness in someone who is a pace-setter is often communication. Such an individual unintentionally aspires to telepathy, expecting the team to guess what the goals, the tasks, and the individual learning needs are. This means that in most teams in most situations the pace-setting style is unhelpful.

Coercive style

Coercive leadership can be highly effective, in short bouts, to meet certain needs. It must be used sparingly and with great care, because it produces a toxic, low-performing environment if employed on a permanent basis. It is useful where people know their tasks, have failed to fulfil them and have no good reason for not having met them. For this, clarity of role and purpose are essential. It is also important that the staff respect the leader entering coercive mode. Greg Lewin, president Shell Global Solutions, defines the parameters:

'I would never use a coercive style on first meeting. I would usually use it when I know that the person knows that they haven't delivered. It is a case of my asking, "Did you really think I'm so stupid that you could pull the wool over my eyes?"

'Also, one should never be coercive unless the standards against which you are judging are very clear; never when it is vague, and never when it is a small issue; never when there is room for misunderstanding. If the rule is you wear a seat belt and on three occasions you haven't then you can be coercive. If the rule is that we start a meeting at 10.00 and for the fourth time in a row someone does not turn up on time then you have to take some action.'

The coercive style can also be of use during a crisis. Generally, fear is corrosive to workplaces if engendered on an ongoing basis, but it can be healthily introduced on occasion to remind people that the world doesn't owe them a living and that the organization has to perform well to survive.

One of the most high-profile coercive leaders of recent years was Al Dunlap, who built up a reputation as a turnaround expert by slashing costs and imposing his will at different industrial firms in the US. When he came to electrical supplier Sunbeam, however, he was taking over a firm whose performance was merely lacklustre, but he proceeded to behave as though it was over-staffed and needed excessive coercion. The results were disastrous: too many staff were fired; motivation plummeted, supplies to retail outlets became irregular and computer errors were frequent. The company hit a financial crisis and the board fired Dunlap.[17]

How to draw up your leadership style chart

The six leadership abilities described above may sound hopelessly vague and subjective, or it may seem that they are the product of innate personality and cannot be learned. Several years of research has now illustrated, however, that they are measurable *and* learnable. You can fill in the questionnaire on management styles on page 69 to give yourself a relative, self-assessed measure. The real test comes when you ask your direct reports to rate you against the same scale. We will discuss some real examples of charts produced by this method, and how they were used to improve personal and business performance, in Chapter 5. You can also test organizational climate with the questionnaire on page 71.

But, before doing that, it's worth discussing how the process works. It is perfectly logical, and illustrated by this simple flow diagram:

Consistent leadership competencies → Complete leadership ability → High-achievement organizational climate → Superior financial performance

Climate is the key measure, and its correlation with success is backed up by research, as you'll see below.

Climate

No style of leadership is neutral. They all have their effect on business performance. As the Sunbeam story noted above indicates, this can even put a company into or close to liquidation.

A telling way of predicting whether business failure is in the pipeline is to check the effect that your leadership style is having on the company. This can be done by measuring climate. Research by Hay has identified the following key features of organizational climate as those that generate better financial returns:

- **Flexibility** – employees in high-achievement climates say that they work in a flexible environment. They feel that their business's leaders are more likely to keep rules to a minimum while promoting innovation.

- **Responsibility** – a high-achievement climate features high levels of responsibility among employees. They are not afraid to take the initiative, and are not always awaiting instruction.

- **Standards** – in the best environments there is a clearly promoted understanding that mediocrity will not be tolerated. This illustrates how, although the more empathic managerial approaches form a part of complete leadership, they should be used to promote high performance, never to let people off the hook. It also shows how the coercive or pace-setting styles may justifiably be deployed on occasion.

- **Rewards** – people in high-performing climates feel well rewarded for their efforts. Their leaders give them constant feedback on their performance.

- **Clarity** – there is a close correlation between clarity of standards and performance expectations in the best-performing teams. Open and free exchange of ideas and information is encouraged.

◆ **Team spirit** – direct reports of the outstanding CEOs say that their organization has high levels of trust, pride and commitment.

You can ask your staff to complete questionnaires on how they feel about the place (see the climate questionnaire, page 71) to generate a relative score on each of the six measures of organizational climate for your team.

The climate of a group or organization has a tremendous bearing on success. While it is not solely determined by the behaviour of the senior leaders, this element is more influential than many realize. Your behaviour influences the climate, which affects performance, which is reflected in results.

A telling way of predicting whether business failure is in the pipeline is to check the effect that your leadership style is having on the company.

One of the most authoritative studies illustrating the links featured the life insurance industry in North America.[18] It found a 'direct link between a high-achievement organizational climate and superior financial performance'. The correlation is very strong. In the study, researchers interviewed 19 chief executives of life insurance companies. These were split into two groups; one of them had achieved good financial performance, and the other outstanding financial performance. The bottom-line returns were judged on four categories: total company capital and surplus growth; ordinary premium growth; first-year recurring premium growth, and general expense ration (see the chart on page 58). As you can see, the gap between the outstanding firms and the others is considerable. Worth having, to put it in the vernacular. Outstanding was defined as being in the top quartile against cross-industry benchmark data. Good performance is defined as being in the second quartile.

The researchers interviewed the two sample groups using standard questionnaires to identify managerial competencies, as described above (see page 55).

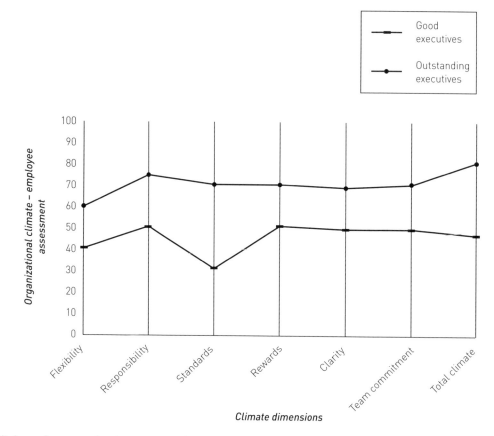

Legend:
- Good executives
- Outstanding executives

Y-axis: Organizational climate – employee assessment (0 to 100)

X-axis (Climate dimensions): Flexibility, Responsibility, Standards, Rewards, Clarity, Team commitment, Total climate

High-performance leaders create a better climate: the organizational climate of outstanding and typical executives from leading life insurance companies
Source: Hay Group

They also carried out in-depth interviews with some 100 direct reports of the 19 executives. This was done in a systematic way, using questionnaires designed to illustrate the organizational climate, and to elicit teams' perceptions of the 19 executives' managerial styles, as described above.

The results were startling. Organizational climate scores were higher in the better-performing companies on all six measures. On 'standards', for example, you can see that the gap was more than 30 percentage points; and on 'responsibility', it was nearly 20. The measure for 'total climate' revealed a gap of just over 20 percentage points.

In the managerial profiles, the coaching and affiliative styles were dominant among the outstanding CEOs, while all 19 showed strong authoritative, democratic and pace-setting styles. Interestingly, none exhibited a strong coercive style. The authors of the report postulate that coercion is of little merit in a fast-changing, mature consumer market like life insurance in North America, where responsiveness and adaptability are needed and staff are highly skilled and mobile. There will be minor differences between industries and companies, but generally the trend in modern economies towards high value-added goods and services produced by highly skilled people with little automatic sense of company loyalty means that there are powerful societal drives rendering coercive styles of management less useful, as we said earlier.

One post-script to the study indicated that managerial attitudes have not entirely caught up with this new reality. All the executives in the study, when asked what were the important leadership attributes, got it wrong. This was true even of the best ones, indicating that they were exhibiting strong coaching and affiliative abilities, but underestimating just how important it was for business success. The researchers found that the following five managerial competencies were most strongly associated with success:

♦ achievement orientation

♦ curiosity and information seeking

♦ change leadership

♦ developing and empowering

♦ listening and responding.

This contrasts with what the executives expected the top five competencies would be:

- strategic thinking
- integrity
- vision communication
- business savvy
- change leadership.

Let's now consider a real-life example of how an inexperienced leader used key managerial styles to develop a young team and yield spectacular business results.

Dave Bennett's story

As director of the international PR firm Manning Selvage & Lee, Dave Bennett heads the division handling PR for technology businesses. Below, there is a fuller profile of how Dave has used authoritative, democratic and coaching styles to grow his division, but first, hear how these styles are reflected in the way he works with two colleagues:

'I recruited my deputy, Nick, through a recruitment consultant. We hit it off personally; his management style is a good complement to mine. He is incredibly knowledgeable about technology. He is a partner rather than a subordinate; I have involved him in aspects of running the practice. The reason it has paid off is that he has always felt empowered to do things. He is now a director as well and we work as co-partners. People do say "Aren't you threatened by him?" I reply that I have never felt threatened, because he is an important part of my success. Jackie (my boss) told me early on in my career that you should always look after people who work with you, and show off how good they are. People say to me [about Nick]: "We admire the way you have brought him on. It reflects well on you." I have seen situations where it is not done and this restricts people. They feel unhappy.

'Another new hire, as an account executive, had only two months' experience, but we liked her. She was very stressed to begin with; was probably not really senior enough for the role that we had given to her, so we took time to work with her and to make sure she was getting the coaching she needed. We were telling her when she was not doing things right, but were encouraging her when she did something well. I really felt a lot of satisfaction when, in almost one day, she went from being someone not hitting deadlines or producing good-quality work, to becoming this machine for producing excellent work. Clients started saying how much they liked working with her. She got great hits in the press. Something just clicked inside.'

The links between these matters of language and behaviour, and real business performance, are more direct than may be apparent initially, and are well illustrated in Dave Bennett's story. Here is an example of some straightforward, learnable managerial behaviour by an individual that directly led to a doubling in turnover for a division of a PR company, and to a strong client base that enabled it to thrive even during the economic downturn. This is an example of the dynamics that the Hay Group and Daniel Goleman's research quantified in determining that 70 per cent of the climate of an organization is determined by leadership behaviour, and that up to 25 per cent can be added to business performance by improving climate. Given that behaviour has such dramatic effects on the bottom line, it does call into question our prejudice in labelling it 'soft'.

Dave's background

New Yorker Dave Bennett, who has worked at Manning Selvage & Lee for ten years, the past seven years in London, was promoted to be acting director on the board at the age of just 30 in 1999, being formally appointed director, with a place on the board, a year later. He heads the technology division, having begun in 1999 with just two staff.

How he learned a key leadership ability

'With one manager I had in New York [early in my career] I would say things like "I'm not senior enough to write a press release," and she would say, "Just do it." It made me more confident. I thought to myself, "When I become senior I will want people to be empowered like this."

'Later, a boss here in the London office was a great role model. We had talked about me taking over the practice and she said, "You have a lot of people around you; you have the ability." These were encouraging words.'

How he applied this ability

'I was there with two other staff, and there was a client opportunity with a video-game publisher. I had a foot in the door, and I wrote to the head of PR. They said, "Come up and see us in Manchester;" they happened to be looking for an agency – that kind of cold-call almost never works. We pitched. They chose another agency but came back to us six months later with a different brief, to do the corporate brand for the UK, not the games.

'I was working on this with just two others – Natasha and Sandrine. The three of us had to pull it off. Probably we needed a couple more. There was always this anxiety: can we actually do it? We didn't have the right mix of people at the time.

'But I got together with them and said that this was our opportunity to make this division grow. Here is a list of what we have to do. We needed to start looking at the brand; how they perceive themselves, and do research. I asked my team: "What are you most interested in doing?" This was instead of saying, "You are only an account executive so you can't do writing." I asked them what they had a passion for. Sandrine said research, and Natasha said writing. So we said that they could do that and gave them some help [with the skills].

'A hierarchy can hold talent and people back. What this enabled us to do was do the work of five people with three of us. The down-side was that I had to do a lot of coaching. These were pretty junior people and I was fairly junior. I had coaching as well [from a senior executive at the firm]. I would say to her, "I have no idea how to do this." She talked me through what she had done, and recommended a brand expert for me to chat with. That made me feel a lot better. I felt, "I can do this."

'We were trying to pitch this company as an up-and-coming French company trying to raise its profile in the UK. Our difficulty was that it wasn't listed, so financial journalists weren't interested. Natasha had the idea of making a star out of the CEO, who is an extremely charismatic individual who gives a great interview. He doesn't really go on-message; he just tells the truth. We thought that we should be using him to get in the door; journalists can meet this guy and get an idea of the fire around the company. Within a year he was on the cover of *Business Week*, he was in *Time* magazine, had a profile in *The Times* and numerous UK publications.

'This all came about from our team-based approach. We were talking about Microsoft; Hewlett-Packard; about [fast-food outlet] Wendy, and about if we had a celebrity CEO, or could make a celebrity, it's a tried and tested way of creating a brand image. You can get the individual too closely tied to the company and in the end the CEO actually asked us to lay off. He was getting recognized in restaurants.

'The fact was, though, that the company was making his promises come true. This all cemented our relationship with the company that continues now.'

How it led to business taking off

'This work led to a Microsoft contract – we do the PR for Xbox in Europe because of the work with the games company. We also did the PR for Disney Online in the UK, France and Germany when it was relaunching.

'We were now able to trade on the work that we had done. We went to similar companies and could say to them, "We can help you out." It led to more business and hiring more people. Suddenly my team was growing. In 1999 technology firms had been between 5 and 10 per cent of the business at the London office of Manning Selvage & Lee. Now [early 2002] it is 25 per cent.'

Income from Dave's technology division had grown from just over £600,000 in 1998 to more than £1m in 2001.

There are three main styles of leadership that Dave Bennett is employing:

- **Authoritative** – at the outset, Dave set a vision for growth in the division and conveyed confidence that the team could realize that vision.

- **Democratic** – Dave involved people, and let them influence the group's direction. This works best when people are already well motivated.

- **Coaching** – Dave helped team members with particular skills, such as knowledge on how to build a brand, or technical skills like writing.

It is clear that the nature of the organization and the team play a part. For example, in industries where health and safety is a dominant factor, such as steel manufacturing or nuclear power, one can't give as much autonomy to junior individuals, because the risks are too great.

Dave had the advantage of staff members who were already highly motivated, so discipline was never a problem. He didn't have to introduce any element of coercion. This is common in the creative industries, where some leaders mistakenly think they are being 'colourful' or 'a character' by throwing their toys out of the pram from time to time. Such childish behaviour is never justified, and the more coercive style is rarely needed in a business where people want to be there and want to do well.

The more coercive style is rarely needed in a business where people want to be there and want to do well.

Contextual factors, however, affect the degree to which one can apply the six different competencies; it is always best to have all six at one's disposal. Dave possesses a strong drive to succeed, and is under pressure himself to deliver returns, so it's likely that he would be capable of resorting to a coercive technique if it were needed; the point here is that it was not. It is also notable that Dave sought to establish a good rapport with his small team, indicating that the affiliative style was employed; he also undertook some of the hands-on work himself, indicating a degree of pace-setting. The three styles highlighted above, however, were the dominant ones.

Emotional intelligence

Added to the six leadership styles, a complete leader will be emotionally intelligent. Much has been written about this concept since it was first defined by Daniel Goleman and others in the 1990s. as discussed in Chapter 2, there can be an unfortunate tendency to write off 'emotional' or personal qualities as being 'soft' or 'pink and fluffy', subordinate to the 'hard' matters of accountancy and strategic analysis. We hope that we convinced you that a choice, or an elevation, of emotional above rational qualities – or vice versa – is not appropriate.

The point in emphasizing emotional intelligence is that it has been traditionally neglected in the development of managers and the MBA curriculum. How we manage people; how we motivate, how we handle the day-to-day negotiations, meetings and politics of real life, is how we manage. It can't be segregated or treated as a junior matter.

Any executive today will tell you of the skills-building courses they have attended. These range from formal academic learning in accountancy, law and business, ranging from cost analysis, calculation of profit margins, structural effectiveness and processes. However, most managers today have received little training or development in empathy, integrity, or how to be an inspiring leader. These are the foundation stones of emotionally intelligent leadership. But research shows that what distinguishes the real leadership stars is still neglected when we build on high flyers' talents. There is still little appreciation that most of us are evaluated by our colleagues, bosses, direct reports and, importantly, by the external stakeholders, including journalists, investors and customers, not only by how 'clever' we are, but also as to whether they like and trust us. Behaviours and habits built around demonstrating empathy, managing self and others, self-awareness, influence and trust are measures that are increasingly being used in hiring and promoting managers.

Alex's story

As Alex was standing in the plush lobby of a building in Mayfair in London's West End, on his way to an interview with a top search consultant, he was shouting down his mobile at his secretary, completely unaware that the receptionist from the firm had crossed the lobby after her lunch break.

His meeting was doomed before it started. The receptionist was friendly and polite when he entered the waiting room, but later went on to warn the headhunter that Alex 'has an awful temper . . .'

Yes, moods are contagious, and no one wants to work for a grouchy boss. We all know how energized we feel when our manager communicates with us, and listens to our concerns and advice. The boss that gave us self-confidence and took our personal and career development seriously will always be remembered.

Alex was also regarded by his team as being rigid, out only for his own good. He was blocked from moving from the regional operational director to the CEO role in his present organization and struggled to come to terms with the fact that the chairman found him difficult to connect with. Despite the fact that he had received this feedback from the personnel director, Alex insisted it wasn't him. After all everyone knew how good his analytical and conceptual skills were. Technically, there was no one to touch him. No wonder he was out in the market looking for the top job if they were not going to promote him. After months on the market and no job offers, he sought the advice of a coach to help him move on.

It took Alex a while to come to terms with the fact that his commanding pace-setting style was not making him well liked in the market. He was known to order people to do things and to criticize them if they didn't do it his way. Slowly, he began to realize how this had been helpful when he had needed to turn around the business in Japan, and then South America; but these had been exceptional circumstances that were unlikely to recur frequently. It began to dawn on him that long-term success was not going to be gained by pushing and firing.

Years of research carried out by Daniel Goleman and the Hay Group provide statistical evidence that emotional intelligence is particularly central to leadership.[19] The more senior your position in the business, the more important political awareness, adaptability, developing others and initiative become. When senior executives derail it's usually because they are defensive, arrogant, moody and insensitive to others' views and needs. They were unable to build teams where co-operation and trust were evident, and were dependent on the coercive and pace-setting management styles.

Decades of research and practical application[20] have convinced us that people can change ... if they want to. It does take an emotionally intelligent approach to recognize that these skills can be learnt. Habits which are now not working for us can be undone, and replaced with new and helpful ones. All it takes is time, practice and motivation.

At 36, ambitious and upset that his career had stalled, having begun so well since graduating from Stamford with an MBA, Alex began to recognize that he needed to change some of his behaviours. It was the concrete evidence and research that convinced him that he needed to do so, and he embarked on the journey with as much energy as other missions in his life. He was not accustomed to losing.

Thinking it would be easy for someone of his intellect and energy, he drew up a series of objectives and plans as to how he was going to make sure he met them. What he didn't want to recognize was how much of an automaton he had become, and how hard it was to shift some of the management routines he had developed. He agreed to learn about the perceptions of others around him and completed a 360-degree emotional intelligence competency. He also asked his team to fill in an upward feedback on management style. Alex was shocked to see how blind he had been. He had relied on integrity and intellect to get him to where he was. He also realized that being sensitive to others was quite easy when things were going well. When he became nervous or tired, especially after long transatlantic flights, he became irritable and had more rows with others. He had also got into the habit of regularly taking sleeping pills with a strong scotch as soon as he got on the flight to help him sleep. No wonder he felt heavy and grumpy when he went straight into the office. He began to take regular breaks and holidays. He hadn't had a day off for 18 months so this was a difficult change for him. He also decided to focus on only two things to start off with, listening and self-awareness. Listening to others was really difficult as mostly he thought he knew the answers anyway. He knew the pay-off was beginning when his secretary seemed less nervous and began to make fewer mistakes. He also began to enjoy the company of his colleagues more.

His coach recognized Alex's talents and strengths and worked with him intensively over a period of six months. Time, effort and practice began to pay off. Helping Alex understand how his behaviour impacted on him, his coach was hugely helpful to him, especially when Alex was unaware how stern he could appear to be. He was beginning to 'rewire' his brain.

It's not difficult to assess one's style, and gauge organizational climate. The following questionnaires can help, and can be repeated after intervals to check progress.

MANAGEMENT STYLE QUESTIONNAIRE

Here are some questions to help you think through what your dominant management style is. Rate yourself on a scale of 0 to 100 on each measure, and ask your team to rate you as well.

1 You believe that a high standard of performance is the most critical theme for success, and you are intolerant of people who do not reach your standards (*coercive*).

Rating _____

2 You believe you have a happy team and that being responsive to how they're feeling is more important than the job at hand (*affiliative*).

Rating _____

3 When you come up with a vision or a decision, you work at inspiring your team to accept it (*authoritative*).

Rating _____

4 The only way to achieve results is by firm discipline (*coercive*).

Rating _____

5 You help people develop by giving them the opportunity to participate and be heard (*democratic*).

Rating _____

6 You discourage people to have arguments, which may lead to conflict (*affiliative*).

Rating _____

7 You often give team members tasks to do but then take them back if you feel they are not performing adequately (*pace-setting*).

Rating _____

8 You lead your team by group consensus and not by directly controlling them (*democratic*).

Rating _____

9 When you discuss performance you focus on assisting people to develop themselves and how to raise their game, rather than on the results themselves (*coaching*).

Rating _____

10 It is important to you that people follow your example (*pace-setting*).

Rating _____

11 If someone's ideas or workplans are not appropriate you help them rethink how they might do it differently (*coaching*).

Rating _____

12 You are able to communicate your ideas and visions effectively and gain enthusiastic support from the team (*authoritative*).

Rating _____

The relative measures on each scale yield useful information in themselves, but don't forget, it's also important to compare your own score with your team's rating of you, to check your level of self-awareness.

THE CLIMATE IN YOUR TEAM

Ask your employees to what degree they agree with the following statements, on a scale of 0 to 100, with 100 indicating complete agreement. Higher scores are generally associated with higher business performance.

Innovation

1 New and original ideas are often implemented in my work group (*innovation vs bureaurocracy*).

Rating _____

2 The people in my team are encouraged to take initiative in solving problems (*initiative vs bureaurocracy*).

Rating _____

Clarity

3 My team are clear about the goals of the business.

Rating _____

4 Practices, policies and procedures are clear to all of the team.

Rating _____

Teamwork

5 The people in my team work well together.

Rating _____

6 People in the unit trust one another.

Rating _____

Reward

7 People are recognized for outstanding performance.

Rating _____

8 We all know who the stars are because they are rewarded for performance.

Rating _____

Standards

9 We are all aware of our standards of performance in the unit.

Rating _____

10 Norms of behaviour and standards are well understood.

Rating _____

chapter four

the picture comes back
from the developers –
how the team sees you

Learning points from this chapter

◆ How your team perceives you is important; it may be different from how you think you put yourself across.

◆ A low score on a key attribute or on self-awareness is not evidence of a character flaw; it is best not to react defensively.

◆ Complete leadership doesn't involve choosing between being directive or democratic but being able to deploy either style, depending on the situation.

We all have our favourite photos of ourselves, where we fancy there is at least a passing resemblance to George Clooney or Julia Roberts. We also have our least favourite, where the hair sticks out, our mouth is set in a grimace, and the lines on our face look like a map of the Rockies.

Yet we probably didn't feel any different when the best and the worst pictures of ourselves were being taken. Behaviour is a little like this. We can have very little awareness of how we come across to others. Our scorecard from the previous chapter may have revealed that when we thought we were being authoritative, really we were being coercive; when we thought we were being democratic, we were being pace-setting. We thought we had communicated well, but actually we expressed irritation at having to tell the team what the plan was, with the result that they felt fearful and did not listen.

As we await the results of the initial feedback, we are in a sense waiting for the picture to come back from the developers. The metaphor may be dated – we live in a digital age without needing to develop photographs on film – but there is always at least a pause before we see how we look in a snap that has just been taken. We can be anxious in that pause.

If you have completed the questionnaires, or you're gathering information from 360-degree or other means, you're waiting for the photograph to come back from the developers. So, how will it be?

It will offer valuable information on your strengths, and your awareness of them compared with your team's perceptions of you. But you may receive some unpleasant surprises. This is to be expected. A low score doesn't indicate a character flaw. If you are not brilliant at everything, that's fine. The key is to think of the things that you can do differently that would make a difference. In Chapter 5, we will set out a '3-D development programme' summarizing your key tasks.

Greg Lewin, president Shell Global Solutions, reports how an incident with a direct report encouraged him to consider how he came across to others:

'With one colleague, his line of the business was being reviewed in a meeting. It is in the nature of these fish-bowl processes (that we have at Shell) that they are high challenge and high support. I looked at the numbers and we looked at cost performance, and the numbers were unacceptable to me. I said "I don't accept your costs," and I meant it as being just that, but he took it as my saying "I don't trust you and I doubt your information." It took a long time for us to reconnect after that. To me it was just an observation. I had misjudged the position that the individual was coming from . . . I could have been much more coaching than challenging.'

This is an example of someone feeling they were being informative, when the direct report felt he was being coerced. What matters here is the subjective perception; that is everything. There is a saying among magazine designers: 'What it is, is what you've done.' This tautology serves to illustrate the futility of arguing, 'Ah, but I was trying for this effect,' if that was not the effect achieved. It can be a hard lesson.

Self-awareness and delegation

Sue Turner, HR director, Group CIO & Functions at Barclays Bank in the UK, comments on how feedback from her team, gathered in a structured way through 360-degree emotional intelligence appraisal, has helped her to delegate, empower her teams and employ 'less assertion; more listening'. She discovered that, though she rated highly on the important attributes, and had good self-awareness – rating herself quite similarly to how her team perceived her, there was something of a gap on two related areas. Her team rated her higher on self-control than she had expected; and a little lower on her ability to express empathy. She realized that her strong desire to achieve by herself, bolstered by nine years' work in the individualistic culture she encountered at Andersen Consulting in the late 1980s and in the 1990s, meant that she had a stronger desire to control tasks than she had realized:

'If there has been a personal leadership journey for me over the last couple of years, it would be about doing less assertion, and a move to a more listening, empathetic approach; and to an approach where I am less scared of leaving things undone.

'I have had an [internal] voice telling me, "I have to do things, otherwise they won't be done right." I have been quite independent, feeling that no one is going to sort my life out unless I do it for myself.

'Without feedback you don't know what you are shifting to and whether it works. My emotional intelligence feedback from direct reports and bosses did contain some surprises. One of the things I found surprising at the time – I had eight or nine direct reports – was the variation in those scores. That comes as a real shock; some scores were either very high or very low [on the same measure]. I thought, "How can this be?" As I went through them one by one I realized that probably the scores bore a direct correlation with the time I spent with people. If there are eight you can't invest as much time as one would want with all of them. The people I spent a lot of time with marked me higher.

'With those with whom I hadn't spent so much time I had assumed that I was being clear, giving good direction and being supportive; that I was listening. Clearly I wasn't (with all my team), but I had convinced myself that I was. This influenced me in how I structured my new team; I kept the number of direct reports down to six.

'The EI survey itself used different criteria. I came high on self-control, and lower than I thought on empathy. On building relationships I scored high. Presence and so on was reasonably high. Overall there was a reasonably good fit between my own awareness and the scores; so there was a match. One that I was surprised at was self-control – that isn't something that I would have singled out; I would have scored myself much lower. I know it's something that I have worked on over the years. In some ways it is encouraging; it does demonstrate that if you can identify something that is blocking your progress or enjoyment then you can find a way of dealing with it.

'I could have [in the past] reacted defensively if someone was criticizing some work that I had done or that my team had done, and gone into justification mode if I didn't agree. I would have been inclined to say there and then what I thought, rather than listen. I would have tended to fight every battle. I can definitely remember operating like this in my early days in Andersen 12 years ago. I can remember being in situations where I could quite easily have an angry outburst with a group of people, because I would have taken something that had happened so personally; I felt threatened and vulnerable. I would have

complete leadership

momentum

assumed that I had to be good at everything – it comes back to being a bit of a perfectionist; I couldn't show weaknesses.

'Over the past couple of years I have begun realizing that you can lead in different ways and can be good at some things and not others. It is OK if you are not good at some things, provided that you explain that you're not. The reaction is not to hurt you with that information but to support you. It all comes back to self-awareness. It is so critical.

'What I have realized is that there are times when people need space, and that to give them space means that they find their own way of coming to a decision. If you give people time to come to a decision on their own, it is a much more powerful decision. The temptation, in a busy, fast-moving environment is to seek instant clarity, and this may not give some people the opportunity to reflect.

'One of the big themes that I have tried to support over the last two years with my team has been getting the team working without me. That is necessary, but I do remember feeling very threatened by the very success of that. I can remember this vividly: we were holding an annual [internal] human resources conference. My natural reaction would have been, "This is so important; I am going to be there with my team, talking about the future and what we need to do. I have to be involved at every stage; being the leader is being out there in front." Then one of the team said, "We're all going to get together next week for a day to work through the conference; everyone's really fired up." I thought, "But I'm not invited!"

'I spoke to another member of my leadership team, who said to me that I have always told them that I want them to work together; that I give them the overall sense of direction and they know what I want. She said that they would play it back [their plan for the conference] the following week. "Trust us," she said. It still felt uncomfortable.

'We had a meeting where they played back an outline of the conference and it was superb. They went through who would do what at which session. I had let them get on with it and they had a great sense of ownership. Momentarily it was frightening. I felt vulnerable: Am I really needed? Luckily, I was able to talk to people around me about how I was feeling, and I was able to put it in perspective.'

Sharing data with the team

One reservation some executives express when it's suggested that they obtain feedback from their staff is whether the team can be bothered to take the time. As we observed at the beginning of this book, though, the boss is important to everyone, and we spend much of each day thinking or worrying about how he or she is or what they may be thinking.

In practice when we ask our teams for feedback some of them agonize over their responses for hours. In nearly all cases they want to help you, at least in part because this will have benefits for them. Most would probably value the opportunity to understand what the feedback did for you, and how you are going to use it for your own personal development plan. Even when you feel vulnerable in view of some of the negative feedback you might receive, this sharing will enable you to build a really strong team. In fact some of the team might like to follow the same data-gathering process for themselves.

Nick had recently moved into a senior management role in a global chemicals company. He took on the job of managing a multinational team of people, many of whom who had been doing their job for over 20 years. Market share and sales had been steadily declining by 5 per cent over a three-year period and Nick was faced with a clear dilemma: replace most of the team or coach them to change the way they work. He decided to have coaching himself after he had been in the role for six months.

When he reviewed the results of the leadership style inventory, Nick's strongest style was democratic. As he was uncertain about what direction to take he felt he needed ideas from the people who had worked in the area for a long time. He put off crucial decisions hoping to get a consensus to a new strategy. He listened carefully to what people were saying; heard their concerns and anxieties and tried to create a sense of collaboration.

What he hadn't realized was that he was seen as a 'ditherer' who lacked focus. As competitors stole more and more customers Nick persisted in running endless meetings to try and get 'buy-in' from the team. So, although everyone rated him as a really nice guy and very empathetic, what Nick now realized was that for the first six months he had mainly used the democratic and affiliative styles, using empathy and coaching and high-emotional self-control. He was popular, but these styles were not enough.

In his work with his coach, Nick realized he had to use a greater variety of management styles. Now that he knew what most of the team were thinking and feeling it was ideal for him to articulate a purpose for the business with clear goals and objectives, both for the team as a whole and the individuals within it. He shared his data from the management style inventory with his team and spent an hour discussing with them what he was going to do more of, and what he was going to do less of. He told them what he was going to change, what he expected from himself and others in the team.

He remembered not to abandon his strengths. His high level of integrity and his likeableness enabled Nick to share the new purpose with his team. They listened. He also shared with them the fact that he was going to use a command and control style more often over the next six months, and why. He explained that he felt that they all had to make some quite drastic changes to the way they were doing things. He recognized that this might be difficult for some people who were resistant to change and the group discussed the consequences to this resistance.

This was not an easy meeting. Despite the high regard in which Nick was generally held, some were unhappy about changing to a higher-paced way of working that reflected the competitive pressure. For Nick, it was contrary to his instinct to employ the coercive style that was needed (though only for the more recalcitrant employees and only on a temporary basis). The coaching and his business awareness had given him a rational case for deploying a more directive approach, and coaching had also helped him with his emotional self-control.

He was deploying an authoritative style with those team members willing to change ('this is where we're going; join me in the mission') and a coercive style with those who were reluctant ('we have no choice but to change; I expect you to meet these targets'). The trick was to use these without abandoning his trustworthiness, and without forgetting that he may need to revert to a more democratic style when the team was better able to set its own direction.

People were clear now about where the business was going and what was required of them. Not all stayed while these changes were happening, but the collective progress was quickly apparent.

Sharing his data with the team helped Nick build a culture of transparency and openness. An important lesson is that the more directive leadership styles – coercive and authoritative – can and should be used in conjunction with feedback from the team and personal development. This illustrates how, as we mentioned in Chapter 2, complete leadership is not 'either' dictatorial 'or' democratic but both, alternately and at times even simultaneously. In a similar way that rational and emotional strands are brought together.

Nick continued to asked individuals regularly for feedback about how they thought he was doing. Although the democratic element was still a strong part of his leadership style, he had learnt to be visionary and coercive too. Six months later, revenues once again took the upwards slope showing 3 per cent growth. Nick also began to use the coaching style more. Thus he began to really develop others through feedback and support.

chapter five

a 3-D image of how we lead – using greater self-awareness to develop leadership strengths

Learning points from this chapter

◆ Drawing up charts based on feedback from employees can yield useful information on leadership.

◆ Personal beliefs and values are important; they can shape behaviours such as workaholism, delegation and trust, and colour how we view gender matters in the workplace, among other key issues.

◆ Building an internal dialogue can help with self-awareness.

◆ Vital insights can come from family and friends, as well as through formal feedback questionnaires.

◆ Feelings are contagious; your mood affects your team's performance.

The feedback obtained in the processes discussed in the preceding chapters will have given you a fuller, more rounded view of yourself, your team, and the areas you need to develop. This part of the book is about making the quantum leap to becoming a complete leader. Before looking at the scorecard that the work gives you, however, it may be helpful to remind ourselves of where this fits in. In the preceding chapters we discussed how leadership can't be 'either' a rational activity 'or' an emotional one. The six management styles that we defined need to be accompanied by both intellectual and behavioural capacities. Too often in business a false comparison is drawn up between 'command and control' approaches to running a business versus democratic and participatory styles. Complete leadership is a participative endeavour; it engages the collective, but it involves direction and authority as well. It is about earning genuine power and using it wisely. To do this we need to ditch the unhelpful polarization of dictatorship and directionlessness.

Complete leadership is a participative endeavour; it engages the collective, but it involves direction and authority as well.

As one business leader, Claire Hall-Moore of Accenture, points out:

'All of these [management] elements need to pull together and it is not always easy to keep the balance between delivery and the people dimension when you are trying to meet some tough targets. Continual feedback is very important, because it may be that in a particular week someone has done something well, and next week they might not be progressing something in the way you want. You need to be telling them what is working and what isn't; they shouldn't have to wait six months to find out at a formal appraisal.'

So now we'll start to put together the ingredients of complete leadership. We can draw up your scorecard.

The charts that the questionnaires produce

We reproduce here some real charts on leadership style and team climate. They are published with the kind permission of Andy Parfitt, controller of BBC Radio 1 in the UK. His case study on how he developed as a leader is related in Chapter 8.

Take a look at Andy's charts on pages 88–91. We can see a high level of self-awareness. On three of the scores of leadership styles – authoritative, affiliative and pace-setting – his own score is near-identical to the way in which his team experience him. He is less

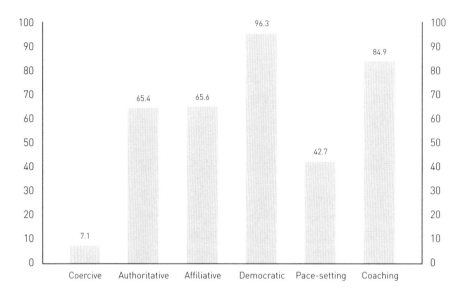

66 = Dominant

50–65 = Backup

Percentiles

Management style inventory (Participant version)

Source: Andy Parfitt, BBC

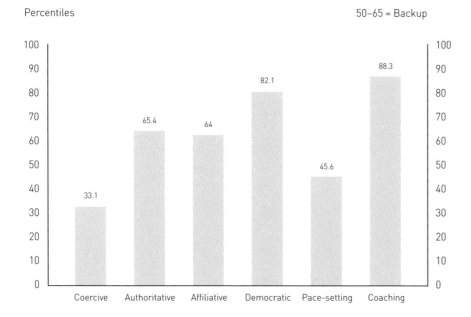

Percentiles

Management style inventory (Employee version (N = 6))
Source: Andy Parfitt, BBC

Percentiles

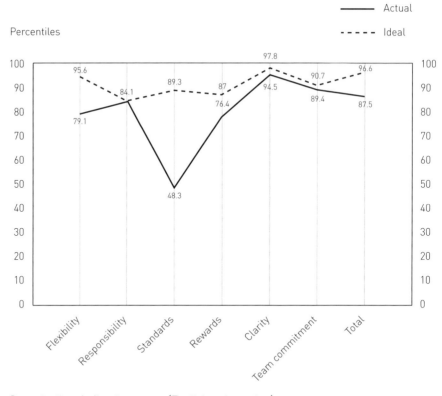

Organizational climate survey (Participant version)
Source: Andy Parfitt, BBC

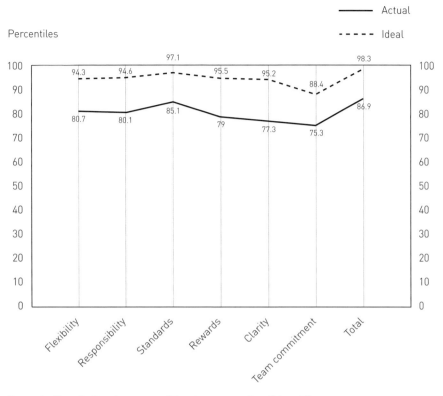

Percentiles

Organizational climate survey (Employee version (N = 6))

Source: Andy Parfitt, BBC

democratic and more coercive than he sees himself; however, this is not a great cause for concern in this particular example. Andy is genuinely supportive of his team – as demonstrated by the high scores he receives under the 'affiliative', 'democratic' and 'coaching' headings. This indicates that he is a 'nice guy' who has made it to the top. For such individuals, the power and status of a senior role are not the main attraction; they value the personal qualities they have retained, and so naturally tend to underestimate the effect that the impact of being 'the boss' has on other individuals. When he suggests that the team does something, he can believe he has been affiliative in style, but because he is 'the controller', at least some of his team interpret it as an order. Hence the higher score under the 'coercive' heading than he would give himself. This is a common dynamic and, provided the gap between the real and perceived attribute in this area is not too great, it is not a cause for concern. Indeed, there is a more even spread of leadership styles in the feedback from his team, than in his own perception; indicating that he is a more balanced leader than he himself realizes.

The coercive style is still low (it probably would have been higher earlier in his realm as controller – see Chapter 8). As indicated in the discussion of the coercive style above, he would probably not want to increase his score here. Andy works in the creative business, for the market leader in popular music radio in the UK, the employer of choice for every DJ in the country. He is not going to be working with people who lack motivation. He is nurturing people with considerable creative talent and in some cases massive egos. This requires intelligence, sensitivity and a good range of emotionally intelligent skills.

Beliefs drive behaviour (and an example of how workaholic beliefs can distort our perceptions)

Beliefs are very powerful things in our lives, and behaviour is organized around beliefs. Often to help us change some of our behaviours we need to examine our beliefs and values systems, otherwise behaviour change is superficial.

It is our contention that everyone possesses beliefs and is guided by them. It is also our contention that beliefs can change. You are not born with them. We have all believed things when we were young which we now look back on and consider rather stupid, and certainly not helpful today. We are not just talking about Santa Claus or the tooth fairy. We can feel embarrassed, for example, about a rather extreme political stance that we adopted while at university.

But some of the most pervasive beliefs that matter to how we manage do not lie within the realm of legend or philosophy or politics, but relate to our views on work, families and careers, some of which we discussed in Chapter 2. Imagine if, for example, you had grown up to believe that all women who are married with children should not work full time until their children leave home. How would you feel then moving into a role where your new boss is a woman with three children all under the age of 11? Or you might believe that people only get somewhere in life by 'working hard' and 'doing it all yourself'. In our experience, we have certainly met many executives who are workaholics and who struggle to build strong teams beneath them.

Poor self-awareness of a pace-setting boss

Bob (not his real name) had a very strong belief that in order to be a successful manager you should be fair and very firm, but certainly not friendly. In fact he believed that if people liked you, found you empathetic, and you took an interest in them and their careers, you were bound to be a 'poor' leader. He developed a management style that was dominantly coercive and pace-setting. He had had feedback over a two-year period that as a partner in a large legal firm more junior professionals were not keen to work with him, despite the fact that he usually sold the most interesting assignments.

His clients thought his work was exceptional, so the firm realized it had to deal with the problem before he hit burnout. To deal with high staff turnover in his team, Bob worked long hours and did a lot of the technical work himself. Most of the time he was exhausted. His management style and climate data showed a large gap in how he perceived himself, and how his team perceives him (see the charts on pages 95 to 100). He saw himself as authoritative and democratic; they saw him as coercive and pace-setting.

To deal with high staff turnover in his team, Bob worked long hours and did a lot of the technical work himself. Most of the time he was exhausted.

Data on the climate and mood he created around him showed low team co-operation, and reward, and poor clarity and standards. No wonder poor Bob had to work so hard. Importantly, Bob had had similar feedback for three years running now and had still not changed. He did try from time to time, but kept slipping back to old habits. Only when he worked through D-3 of the 3-D model (see page 107) was he able to reframe his beliefs and begin to work on changing his behaviour. Not only did the performance in his team improve but contribution of his team to the profits margin of the firm increased by 8 per cent.

The charts we have discussed of Andy Parfitt and of Bob give a vivid and comprehensive picture of our level of self-awareness derived from a relatively simple questionnaire process. Remember, this is an established process, not just a theory, and it has been used to help thousands of managers improve their performance. They show how Andy had a strong level of self-awareness and that, initially, Bob did not. The point to emphasize here, however, is that self-awareness is an improvable ability, like any human skill. Bob had the integrity and honesty to work hard on this aspect of himself; specifically confronting his deeply embedded belief, which he had probably carried since childhood, that empathy and friendliness were incompatible with leadership. This belief had stymied his self-awareness and his growth as a leader. It had caused him to consider himself more authoritative than was experienced by his team, but he did possess the courage to challenge this belief, leading to the improved performance of his team, and ultimately to better business results.

Percentiles

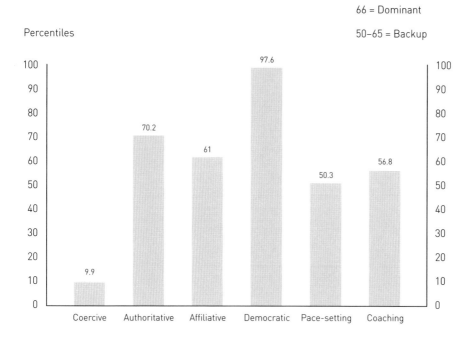

Management style inventory (Participant version)
Source: Hay Group, 2002

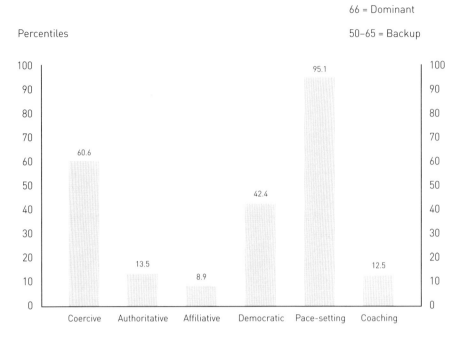

66 = Dominant

50–65 = Backup

Management style inventory (Employee version (N = 6))

Source: Hay Group, 2002

66 = Dominant

50–65 = Backup

Percentiles

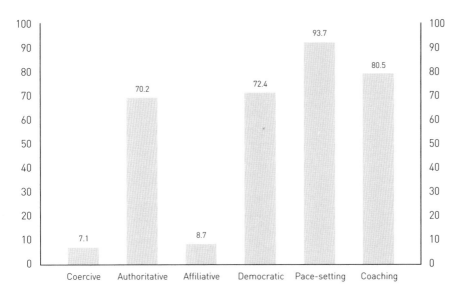

Managerial style inventory (Participant version)

Source: Hay Group, 2002

Percentiles

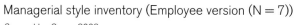

10.5	19	9.3	41.3	90.3	10.7
Coercive	Authoritative	Affiliative	Democratic	Pace-setting	Coaching

Managerial style inventory (Employee version (N = 7))

Source: Hay Group, 2002

Percentiles

Actual
---- Ideal

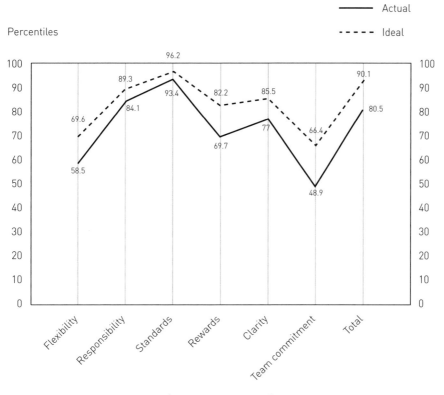

Organizational climate survey (Participant version)
Source: Hay Group, 2002

Actual ——————

Ideal - - - -

Percentiles

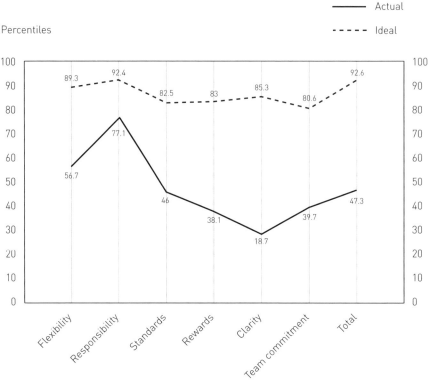

Organizational climate survey (Employee version (N = 7))

Source: Hay Group, 2002

What Bob did was to develop a better dialogue with himself. He
acknowledged his internal voices – the commonest of which we
discussed in Chapter 2 – which are often so familiar to us that we
don't recognize how loaded or even extreme they may be. Internal
dialogue is something that everyone engages in, but people who are
more self-aware have developed a more conscious process. They
know what they are saying to themselves and they can improve and
correct the messages. There has been recent research on brain activity
patterns indicating a strong correlation between inner speech and
self-awareness. One researcher, Dr Alain Morin of Quebec
University, concludes:

'I suggest that the brain regions involved in self-awareness are identical to the regions responsible for inner speech. This can be taken as additional evidence of a link between self-talk and self-focus.'

Crucially, for the purposes of our discussion here, one of the many psychological studies that Dr Morin cites involved participants engaged in comparing themselves against adjectives describing certain human traits – very similar to the questionnaires that create the management style charts we show in this chapter.[21]

Strong differences between how we think we are and how others see us can have at their root damaging internal voices, as discussed in Chapter 2. Hence the importance of recognizing the links between the way in which we see ourselves and the way in which we talk with ourselves.

Internal dialogue is something that everyone engages in, but people who are more self-aware have developed a more conscious process.

Some leaders are naturally reluctant to spend too long 'navel gazing'. Indeed, at its extreme, too much absorption in how we come across can result in excessive self-consciousness, feeding doubt, indecision and too much distraction from the outside world. But note the stress here on the word 'positive' as well as the word 'dialogue'. The purpose of this exercise is to improve organizational performance, not simply engage in the fun process of learning about ourselves. It's a question of being aware of our strengths and weaknesses, telling ourselves about the strengths and building on them, making the links between these, the reaction of our teams, how they perform and hence how the business performs. As we said in Chapter 2 we learn more from what we do well than we do from our mistakes, but it's difficult to learn from either if we don't know what they are.

Again, it's worth repeating that our demeanour, attitude and behavioural styles have an impact on the organization whether we recognize this or not.

When all else fails, ask your kids

As work pressures become intense, it's tempting to follow the old advice: 'If you are feeling stress, tension and a headache, do what it says on the medicine bottle: take two and keep away from children.' But if you can resist this temptation, the advice and feedback from your children, if you have any above toddler age, will be valuable. It is safer to hear from your daughter that you pull a face when impatient or bored, than it is to hear from the boss of a corporate client explaining a contractual detail. Or rather, the corporate customer will not tell you, but simply take the business elsewhere.

The purpose of this exercise is to improve organizational performance, not simply engage in the fun process of learning about ourselves.

Our view of how we are comes not only from formal appraisals. It is worth asking our partner and friends how we are – little or major things from whether we get cross when we can't find our way while driving, to how we express anger over a personal conflict, or how we set about making major life decisions. As in the workplace, there can be surprises. Many people have experienced hearing from a friend, 'Cheer up, it might never happen,' when in fact they were feeling perfectly cheerful. So, how often do we *appear* miserable in the board meeting, without realizing it? What impact does this have on the chairman? On our chances of promotion?

Those with teenage children probably have the richest source of honest feedback on how we come across. Think about it: who is more intelligent, less guarded, more savvy but also, crucially, more desperately wanting to admire and respect you and to care about how you come across? Mothers have known for generations that when they are really unsure about whether their dress is suitable, they ask their 16-year-old daughter, because she will strike just the right balance between trendy and mature. It is the same with behaviour. Just as they will be the first to warn you not to dance at the wedding disco, even if your favourite Motown classic is playing, they will also advise you on more formal matters. If, for example, you have just given a talk at a family occasion, or a school event, ask your children how you came across. Were you a touch on the arrogant side, or too diffident? Did you exhibit any nervous habits such as fiddling with your fingers or stroking your hair? Be prepared for honesty.

One executive was forever being told by his staff, informally and through appraisals, that he did not listen. He was reluctant to believe the finding in itself, or to acknowledge its importance even if it were true. Then he had a long drive with his family on the way to the summer holiday. Six hours later, with his wife at his side and his teenage children behind him, he learned that his family had a problem with him. 'You don't listen to us, Dad,' the children informed him. He started to take his staff's attitudes more seriously after that, and his relations with his team improved. So did their performance.

Feelings are contagious (you can make others feel really good or really bad about themselves)

The boss's secretary warns you: 'I wouldn't go near him today if I were you.' She wrinkles her nose as her face adopts a little grimace. She shakes her head slightly. Unfortunately, you have the misfortune to be called to his office, and leave feeling miserable just ten minutes later.

All of us have at one time or another experienced something like this. On the other hand, there are times when you were feeling miserable and a colleague or team member or (who knows) even the boss, has cheered you up. Our moods affect those around us to a far greater degree than is commonly supposed.

Our moods affect those around us to a far greater degree than is commonly supposed.

Students of psychology learn this early on. Consider the following recollection:

'In my second year studying for a BA in psychology I remember taking part in an experiment where I was placed in a chair in front of a person I didn't know. I also didn't know that he had been instructed to frown and grimace at me and look bored for five minutes. Neither of us were allowed to speak or gesture in any way. It was a very long five minutes and I felt really upset afterwards. The next day I was placed in front of someone else who smiled at me for five minutes. We ended up laughing and I was really sorry when the five minutes were up. We became really good friends afterwards.'

There is science to back this up. Daniel Goleman writes:

'A growing body of research on the human brain proves that, for better or worse, leaders' moods affect the emotions of the people around them. The reason for that lies in what scientists call the open-loop nature of the brain's limbic system, our emotional centre . . . We rely on connections with other people to determine our moods. Research in intensive care units has shown, for example, that the comforting presence of another person not only lowers the patient's blood pressure, but also slows the secretion of fatty acids that block arteries.

'The same holds true in the office, boardroom, or shop floor; group members inevitably "catch" feelings from one another. In 2000, Caroline Bartel at New York University and Richard Saavedra at the University of Michigan found that in 70 work teams across diverse industries, people in meetings together ended up sharing moods – both good and bad – within two hours.'[22]

It is possible that not all moods are equally infectious. One study, by the Yale School of Management in 1999, indicated that fun and laughter catch on more readily than irritability, which in turn was more infectious than depression.

The one important caveat is that the positive mood that a leader attempts to inculcate in the team must be genuine. After all, if a grinning executive who has just made a series of redundancies and cashed in some lucrative share options begins talking about how great the company is, this is not going to prompt the staff in the cubicles to start whistling, 'Oh, What a Beautiful Morning' and go home with smiles on their faces.

Complete leadership involves appreciating all of the influences on an organization; from the cash in the bank, to the views of the customers, to the attitudes of the staff towards the pay scheme, to the technical ability of the operational managers, and so on. The personal attributes that we encourage you to develop in this book need to be grafted on the real you, working in a real organization, with an awareness of the three-dimensional world around you. These matters all affect you, and you affect them.

3-D development

With a fuller appreciation of how we come across, we are better placed to begin improving our complete leadership skills. To provide an easy-reference guide, we conclude the self-awareness programme and begin the development with an approach that we call '3-D development'.

This approach bears similarities to the 'balanced scorecard' technique used at an organizational level, where measures across a range of business assets and features are involved.

3-D development is focused more closely on the leader and the leader's team. The aim is to ensure that development and coaching is focused and measurable, especially in terms of its impact and contribution to the business. This can ensure that the bigger picture is taken into account in a systematic way, connecting business and individual performances. It may sound rather general, but it is remarkable how quickly such an approach can be used to tease out practical issues and develop specific solutions, as we'll see below.

3-D development creates a framework for individuals and teams to benchmark their own progress as the demands on them grow and change in line with business needs. The process seeks to align individual perceptions and the abilities of managers into the business strategy, ensuring that the impact of individuals and teams are interlinked with business performance. Coaching on its own focuses on an individual. As we noted in Chapter 2, investors are increasingly looking for systematic ways to gauge leadership ability, and for robust leadership development and succession planning programmes.

Remember, when using 3-D – or any form of balanced scorecard approach – always ask yourself the following questions:

◆ Is the goal specific?

◆ Is the goal measureable?

◆ Is the goal time-phased?

◆ How will you know when you have reached your goal?

◆ How will others recognize that you have reached your goal?

◆ What obstacles in yourself or in your environment may hinder your attempt to reach your goal?

◆ Who or what can be a source of help to you in reaching your goal or in overcoming possible obstacles?

The 3-D approach equips you with a mapping language that you and your team (and your boss if you have one) can agree, and which is clear and understood by all parties. This should include a full brief of the business, strategy, pressures and demands.

THE 3-D DEVELOPMENT MODEL

D-1 Do what you do well even better – remember you can even improve on your strengths. Give yourself permission to excel in the skill that you are best at, which is likely to be the one you enjoy most.

D-2 Determine what needs to change – think of the things that you could do differently that would make a difference. Remember: this has to be actions, not just thoughts.

D-3 Define the values – those values that support or block you in becoming a complete leader. Internal voices may persuade you that you cannot be number one, or that 'nice people cannot be leaders'.

THE 3-D QUESTIONNAIRE

1 List your strengths: all the things you are really good at.

Now check these with your boss, a colleague or direct report. Even your partner at home may help you. Think about how you might do them even better.

2 Now list some of the things you are not really good at.

Stand back and think what you might do differently to be more effective. Again you might wish to check these out with your boss, a colleague or direct report.

The questionnaire processes on leadership styles and organizational climate described in Chapter 3 will also give information on D-1. If you have followed these, and particularly if you have supplemented this process with informal methods of gaining feedback about how you lead, you will have a good idea of your strengths and weaknesses. You know the 'real me'.

Then examine D-2, to identify what you and the team could do to be more effective in doing what the business really needs. This creates a second list – the 'desired me'. In this way you are beginning to understand how effective you are and can plan how you might add new dimensions to cope with future demands.

For example, Shelley, the finance director of a financial services company, had a terrific grasp of what was going on in the company, but not much understanding of what she regarded as peripheral matters affecting her and her colleagues' success. She saw herself as a finance director only and didn't believe in spending time talking to investors or the press, seeing this as the domain of the chairman and chief executive.

This turned out to be an expensive view to take. Investors became nervous that they were not getting the full story and the press became suspicious. What should have been an innovative acquisitions policy became derailed because of a falling share price.

Investors and shareholders today are constantly examining the calibre of today's and tomorrow's leaders. Succession planning is scrupulously reviewed. To be successful, complete leaders may have to 'unlearn' old and favoured ways of doing things. A systematic approach to identifying strengths and weaknesses, such as the 3-D approach outlined here, can help you to do that. It will help you pinpoint where you need to boost your skillset matched against the company's short- and long-term objectives, and can particularly help in areas where you feel 'stuck' and struggling to change. Directors and key players are now being assessed as to whether they have the flexibility to master different management styles, and what they need to do to be successful. The balanced scorecard, and our particular application of it here, is a process that not only helps business processes, but can also help you and your team to be complete leaders.

Take the case of Harry, who was the finance director of a medium-sized clothing retail company. He was happy at work and his wife was expecting their first baby in January, in six months' time. The business was doing well and the initial founders were happy with his work. Change was forced on Harry when a new CEO was brought into the firm to grow the company through acquisition. The original owner/founder moved into the role of non-executive chairman.

Harry was beginning to feel overworked. Long hours were draining him of enthusiasm, and exhaustion was beginning to set in. Challenge from his coach to delegate more to his team and rethink the way he was working was rebuffed. 'They're not up to it,' he would say. 'And anyway, they're also overworked so it wouldn't be fair.' Harry had always seen his role as collecting accurate data from the retail outlets and presenting it at board meetings. Then of course there was budgeting, and forecasting, but he was convinced that *only he* could do all of that.

Harry's coach worked with him through the 3-D model. He was clear about his strengths: honesty and integrity, capacity for hard work, ability with figures, and knowledge of the business. What he was less clear about was what he needed to change.

After some reflection and encouragement from his coach he realized that he needed to strengthen his team and delegate some of the more routine work to them. The results from tests of his emotional competence startled him. He realized he was not seen by his team as displaying empathy or as taking initiative. They also resented the fact that he didn't enable them to develop, but was seen as controlling and interfering. His relationship with the new CEO was somewhat fractious at times and Harry knew now that he would have to work at that too. He recognized that he needed to communicate with him far more regularly and openly.

All his pressures and challenges were interlocked. His long hours were the result of priding himself on his capacity for hard work in the finance role, combined with difficulty in handling a demanding boss, and his disinclination to delegate to his team. The phrase 'vicious circle' – or 'circles' – came to mind. The deeply rooted nature of his dilemmas made them seem daunting, but there was one tremendously liberating realization: the route out of them lay in his hands. What appeared to be an unchangeable environment was actually caused – at least in part – by his decisions and his behaviour. This could be changed.

What appeared to be an unchangeable environment was actually caused – at least in part – by his decisions and his behaviour.

When reviewing the D-3 in the model, Harry realized that the root of the problem was that he really believed, 'It will only ever be right if I do it myself.'

So what 'pushed' Harry to change? No doubt Sam, the new baby, had something to do with it. He was determined to see him every morning for at least half an hour and to bathe him in the evening. This meant that he had to change the way he worked and reframe some of the perceptions that had ruled his life until now. He spent dedicated time with the four key members of his team and took them through a similar coaching process to the one that his coach had taken him through. They were delighted to be given more responsibility, but recognized this meant that they were clearly accountable for the work they produced.

Harry began to spend more time with investors to explain the company's strategy. Presentations of the half-yearly results were well received, and the share price responded positively. He took an active part in changing the way he and the CEO worked, and communicated with him regularly both in a formal and informal way during the week. He was overwhelmed that his boss was delighted to receive regular updates while he was sailing around the Turkish coast.

Importantly the 3-D model helped Harry rethink who he was and how he wanted his life to be. He is excited by the fact that he and little Sam have bonded so well. His job has moved on from being routine to being a constantly changing one. He has managed two acquisitions over the last eight months, and is the 'darling' of investors and journalists. But he has retained the 'real' Harry – the one who is full of integrity, and who really believes in what and how he is doing. He regularly asks his team and some of his colleagues for feedback. He knows he has more work to do with his boss and some of the managing directors. He feels he has grown another six inches.

The level of self-awareness that we have encouraged you to develop in this chapter is grounded in the discipline of gathering feedback from the people you work with. With this realistic grasp of how you are in your real-life context, we have introduced a systematic way of beginning development that is rooted in the real you and in your real business environment.

We move in the next chapter to the task of personal development, exploring the barriers to overcome and discussing some of the methods, such as coaching, that can help.

chapter six

so, I'm not perfect – what next? the development begins in earnest

Learning points from this chapter

♦ It is important to test and measure your improvement.

♦ Your colleagues and direct reports have competing commitments.

♦ Unspoken assumptions can sabotage brilliant plans.

♦ Intelligent people can support illogical ideas.

♦ Some notes on how to deal with time pressures.

♦ Look after yourself!

♦ Coaching can help, but there are pitfalls.

This chapter in some respects addresses the crunch point: you have improved self-awareness; better knowledge of areas you need to develop and a map for how you might effect this. Now it's time to start improving.

Greater awareness of how we actually are as leaders – how we come across to others – helps us develop in the areas where we are strong and to remedy weaknesses. It forms the basis for continual improvement.

The case study that follows provides a graphic example of the challenges and achievements that can come through changing managerial styles and behaviour. It involves the use of a personal coach; however, we hope by now you recognize that the key to the process of recognizing the importance of leadership skills, increasing self-awareness and developing a more complete leadership style – which can be achieved with or without a coach. You will see that this individual was in quite an isolated position, and the appointment of a personal coach helped overcome that.

Robert's story – integration of intellect and emotion: conquering workaholism

When Robert moved into the role of CEO in an international financial institution, he realized that his new job was much more complex than he originally believed. He was struggling not only with the diverse views on strategy and objectives among the executive team, but also with the strong political undertones. He was trying to think of all the things he had learnt both on the job and in courses and programmes over the past few years, but found it difficult to pull all the pieces together. It was after a particularly difficult board meeting that the HR director, who was a member of the top team, suggested that he might like to do some work with an executive coach. At first, Robert felt that he was being criticized and was annoyed by the suggestion. After all it was 'tough going' at the top and everyone knew that. As was the case with the CEO Jeremy (Chapter 1), he knew someone in his previous organization who had been working with a coach and who'd then been redeployed, so he associated coaching with failure. Robert knew little directly about coaching, and was not aware that, as a distinct intervention, executive coaching remains poorly defined.

Over a drink later in the evening with Mike (the HR director) he began to understand what executive coaching was and how this process could help him pull together and embed some of his learning from the past few years. He saw how it might link his personal development with his own performance and results. He also began to recognize how the process could help him understand how he might get the best out of himself and his team. Mike explained the process, methodology and the confidentiality aspects. He suggested that after he had met with his coach Robert share some of the aspects of his meeting with his team. This would build up values of trust and transparency. Robert was surprised to learn that many of the top team had indeed worked with coaches in the past and that 25 were still actively engaged in coaching throughout Europe. This had been initiated alongside the executive development programme that the company had run with the Paris-based business institute INSEAD four years previously.

Robert is not the only senior executive who has felt anxious about moving into a new job. In a survey on leadership in new roles only 55 per cent of managers who had moved into new roles felt adequately prepared (see Chapter 1). Robert also recognized that he should have taken the time to understand the politics of the organization at the top, especially in view of the fact that he had relocated from Chicago to Manchester in the UK. Like many of the respondents in the survey Robert, born and brought up in the US, missed some of his friends and colleagues whom he had seen regularly. His wife and children seemed to be settling down well, but they too were missing their cousins and other close family members. His mentor had retired, and he found that he actually had no one to talk to.

In the same survey cited, only 58 per cent of new leaders felt clear about their job and only 19 per cent felt that they were very satisfied with what they had been able to achieve. Many felt stressed, and felt that in order to be successful they would need to display some defined leadership skills and behaviours. When Robert read the list, which included influencing across organization boundaries, top team development, creating and articulating a vision, some alarm bells began ringing in his head. He realized, like many other executives, that he would need to spend more time reflecting on his new role, and to take more time to understand the complexities of the organization and its structure and culture in the round. Importantly, he had begun to learn from financial reporting systems that the business was not doing as well as he had initially thought.

When he met with his coach he was impressed by his strong track record. The coach's challenging questions helped him articulate some of his concerns in a surprisingly short time. He found his coach incredibly insightful. The 'safe house' environment where he was asked questions, given advice and even given wise counsel was already starting to be valuable. He saw how, in partnership with his coach, he could identify a set of goals which would improve both his professional performance and personal satisfaction. Robert loves sport, and he found that it helped to draw comparisons between his own coaching and that of other high-performance individuals, such as Tiger Woods and David Beckham, who continue to receive coaching to improve their performance even when they are at the top of their game. Why, he wondered, had he associated coaching with failure and poor performers?

What surprised Robert most was how focused and measured his coaching was – and how closely linked to business success. He had imagined that it would be a series of nice cosy chats that might make him feel a little better but not be directly helpful. By his second meeting, he and his coach agreed on how they would gather feedback data from people about his leadership style. Initially, 180-degree feedback and focused interviews helped Robert understand how he was perceived. He reviewed his six leadership styles and was upset that his team saw him as being apprehensive about delegating, expecting immediate compliance. He had assumed that his strong democratic style which had been his strong trademark as director of operations had prevailed. What his coach helped him to understand was that, when he felt under pressure or lacking in confidence, he tended to become a pace-setter with little sympathy for poor performance. He recognized that this was beginning to demoralize not only some of the members of the board, but their teams as well.

He and his coach followed a definite process in their coaching. They both agreed that he had to raise his self-awareness, so that he would recognize how people actually felt about him. He needed to learn to listen to peoples' opinions, feelings and value statements as well as facts and figures. Importantly, he began to learn about how an American might be viewed in corporate headquarters in the UK, and to stop comparing Manchester to Chicago.

In reviewing the feedback about the climate he was creating, Robert agreed with his coach that he needed to articulate a clear vision for the team as well as the business. He had neglected to create a culture of clarity, accountability and team commitment. In addition, people with initiative were often pushed 'back into their boxes', ensuring that bureaucracy was rife. New and innovative thinking was clearly not rewarded. It had taken a while for him to realize that people still clung to their functional silos, and valued pleasing their bosses more than pleasing their customers. Clearly, his ambition to be a great CEO would require, more than anything else, changes in values, practices and relationships throughout the company. People had to learn to collaborate and to develop a team sense of responsibility for the performance of the business. The links between his personal development, the nurturing of teamwork, and the service to customers – the source of all profits, after all – became more prominent and more clearly defined in his mind.

Robert began to think about what his strengths were and how he could identify other areas where they might be applied. This began to build his self-confidence, especially when he acknowledged his credentials and achievements. He used his ability to think strategically and conceptually, not only in operations, but also in aligning operations more powerfully with marketing. Marketing and operations were beginning to speak together in a different way, and operations staff were beginning to focus on the customer. He also looked at ways that he might become more effective and how he needed to change some of his behaviours. He knew he had to 'let go' and really develop and empower others. Why then did he still continue to check up on his managers, and why did he often cut others off in mid-conversation? His coach also helped him think about how some of his values were stopping him from changing. Why did he still think that 'hard' work was still the only way to the top? No wonder others thought he was a workaholic and his wife and kids complained they never saw him. Also, he had to stop evaluating the performance of the senior management population by the number of hours they worked.

After two meetings, Robert and his coach had engaged in a clear partnership relationship. Their contract was clear and they had agreed measures and outcomes. Robert not only began to think differently about himself and his role, but people noticed that he was listening more, and was clearer about his expectations of the performance of others. Importantly, by listening to others' concerns and views, he took people with him, rather than leaving them abandoned at the bottom of the hill.

The process that they were following in the coaching programme was clear. There had been a first phase of 'review', now they were in the second phase of 'reshaping', and would soon be moving into the phase of 'relearning', and embedding these learnings. He examined some of his values and assumptions, and saw how some of these were making life difficult for him and his team. He had always firmly believed that, if you want things done well, 'you have to do them yourself.' Now he realized how this was stopping him to empower and trust others. He suddenly saw how the team in Brussels had felt when he had started redoing things they had done. Their frustration with his behaviour had seemingly sucked the oxygen out of the room. No wonder they seemed to have no energy when they were in meetings. It became clear to him how he needed to engage with them yet 'back off' as well.

Between meetings Robert's coach tasked him with a number of exercises to work on. This was to help some of the new behaviours stick. He began to be able to evaluate his own behaviour in meetings and really look for evidence that what he was doing was successful. He thought about how he had upset Ruth, the finance director, only three weeks after she had returned from maternity leave by going on about her commitment to the business. It was obvious she could no longer work weekends and evenings, yet that was what he had come to expect her to do before her son was born. In fact, could he expect it from *anyone* on a regular basis?

It goes without saying that the lives of executives are frequently overwhelming, complex and difficult. There are daily opportunities for significant failures in their job performance and personal situations. Most muddle through with little or no external assistance except what's available from colleagues, family or friends. Coaching, as Robert learnt, provided him with an additional safety net. He and his coach had embarked on an intensive and complex commitment to the path of growth. They had built up a relationship of trust, mutual respect, genuineness and authenticity.

Importantly during the relearning phase, Robert began to make sense of the six-week programme he'd attended at Stamford the summer before he moved into the top job. He made real links between business strategy, market focus, and revenue growth and his own capability to deliver these, as well as with that of the global teams. Through the challenging discussions with his coach, what he needed to continue to do to be successful became clearer. He saw how the collection of evaluation data from instruments and interviews, the creative and effective use of levels of reflection and methods of inquiry, and the application of such techniques as role-playing, reframing, simulations, confrontations and interpretations in a timely and sensitive way had all constituted the foundation of his leadership journey. He saw how he had made steady progress towards the goals he and his coach had established in phase one. Coaching was beginning to pay off.

As well as addressing the specific goals and potential long-term barriers in his leadership journey, Robert became dedicated to the idea of continuous learning for all aspiring managers in the business. He realized how being aware of his own skills, his strengths and weaknesses, and having a plan as to how to enhance his performance was benefiting the business. He saw how keeping pace with changes meant re-inventing some parts of himself. Benchmarking and updating his own skills as well as those of the senior team meant that they were not only beginning to respond to change but anticipating it as well.

He saw how people were beginning to move across regional and functional boundaries and that they were becoming much less defensive. He saw how the systematic process of taking stock of those attributes that influenced his own effectiveness, success and happiness had reduced his own anxieties. Coaching had given him a shot of reality and put things in perspective.

Having come up through an operations route, Robert had been sceptical about coaching from the start. He had not realized that the assessment data would provide such a solid basis for setting stretch goals and measures for his leadership journey. He was engaged by the contracting process because he always needed concrete evidence and measures to 'prove' things were going in the right direction. He managed his time differently to make sure he had time to think through and prepare himself for most meetings, and to integrate his 'intellectual' management learning with the 'emotional' management learning. Role-plays and challenges from his coach had enabled him to review things from different perspectives, to take risks and be himself. His team felt more relaxed in his presence and more energized by his ideas.

Working with an executive coach had helped Robert learn that he could not be expected to know all the answers, bear all the load and do all the work. Investing his time and soul in trying to understand what true leadership was all about enabled him to develop a learning strategy.

I need to change . . . Some notes on 'competing commitments'

As the case above illustrates, the route to effecting lasting change in leadership behaviour is not straightforward.

A common experience is the following: you accept the challenge to improve; you are fired up to achieve it. You accept that you must communicate with your team more, for example, or that you will respond to an individual's failings with some extra coaching, rather than with a scolding or by setting an even tougher challenge. Conversely, you may need to give more direction and discipline to a wayward and aimless team and enforce the norms and expectations more clearly.

But your initial efforts seem to fail. You have explained to a manager who reports to you the benefits – both business and personal – of her establishing a network with her equivalent managers in other divisions of the company around the world. You know that they can save money and time by swapping ideas on the use of technology or more efficient ways of operating. She will learn and boost her promotion prospects from the exercise. You arranged for a training course to help her set this up. Drawing on the communication skills you have developed, you remembered to set aside time to explain the rationale fully to the manager, rather than just fire off an e-mail or give instructions in a terse manner.

Yet, despite the fact that she is intelligent, dedicated and hard-working, she still has not set it up. Both of you seem stuck: your coaching style is not working and your colleague is not developing either.

Firstly, take note: this is a common phenomenon. What on earth is going on? Stay patient, though, because exploring the dynamics at work here can assist both you and the person who reports to you.

The explanation lies in recognizing the extent to which each of us as individuals is 'wired' in certain ways. What this means is that while a human being has an unknowable capacity to change and improve, each of us has deeply ingrained patterns of behaving that have built up over years or decades and often exist for good or inescapable reasons.[23] We have strong internal voices prohibiting some forms of behaviour, including some that would be helpful to us. It is important to remember that we all have these.

We have strong internal voices prohibiting some forms of behaviour, including some that would be helpful to us.

As Daniel Goleman and others have persuasively argued, and as we discussed in the last chapter, behavioural wiring is more difficult to reconfigure than knowledge-based wiring. By the time we are in our 20s our range of emotional skills, our way of being in the world, have some strongly set patterns. The more we exhibit them, the more entrenched they become.[24] This is why developing self-awareness, through gaining feedback from the people around us, is so important.

Understanding these dynamics is important both for yourself as a leader and for appreciating the motivations of your direct reports. It informs why we sometimes don't come across to others as we would wish; and also why others don't behave as we expect. Without the development of self-awareness, the manager who is, for example, reluctant to set up a team that would actually help him and the organization is probably obeying a deeply buried mental instruction, as we have discussed in earlier chapters. It could be, for example, that she was brought up to think that 'sharing knowledge makes you vulnerable.'

Researchers Robert Kegan and Lisa Laskow Lahey have recorded how managers often defeat their own objectives by being unable to break out of the limits that some of these mental instructions give them. For example, they may wish to empower their teams and delegate more so that they tap the skills of the team to a better extent and relieve their own workload, but they have a perfectionist and individualistic internal voices telling them, 'I have to do everything by myself,' which is generally rooted in childhood. This means that the temptation to intervene in the way a direct report is handling a delegated task is too great, so they take over some of the tasks, with the effect that the employee is demotivated and the leader is overburdened once more.

Kegan and Lahey call these distracting voices 'competing commitments'. They have established questionnaires that tease them out, and use the information gained as a basis for exploring these commitments and beginning the behavioural change that overcomes their more negative effects. Our programme of continual assessment and monitoring of self-perception, team perception, and business climate aim to do the same.

In a similar fashion, it is now a well-observed phenomenon that intelligent people can support illogical ideas. They use their intelligence to construct ever more elaborate defences of a position to which they have an emotional attachment – for example, they feel they would 'lose face' by admitting the error of a position adhered to earlier. This is common in politics, particularly of the more ideological kind. The great writer George Orwell once constructed a list of blatantly untrue statements passionately adhered to by members of different political movements, including intellectuals. He commented that the individuals would probably never doubt their beliefs 'even in their most private thoughts'.[25]

This also occurs in management, where individuals can, for example, become overly attached to a particular initiative or reorganization, and they filter out information indicating that it is mistaken. Management researchers Heike Bruch and Sumantra Ghoshal observed this in their study of managers at German airline Lufthansa in the 1990s:

'Even though the entire industry faced a severe downturn and Lufthansa was losing revenue, these managers ignored or reinterpreted market signals, convincing themselves that the company's expansionist strategy was correct. Many of them continued to hire new employees in the face of massive operating losses.'[26]

For these and other reasons, getting into the habit of gaining continual, honest feedback from the real world of your customers and your team is a powerful tool in the process of becoming a complete leader.

How different is your colleague?

An important element is to recognize that a colleague's instincts and internal voices are likely to differ strongly from yours, even if superficially the person appears to be of similar temperament and background. There is a growing body of literature and research on the challenges of managing multicultural teams; of recognizing that the 'taken for granted' assumptions about manners, leadership, teams and similar matters, can differ sharply between different nations. Help on this matter can be obtained from consultancies such as Trompenaars Hampden Turner Inter-Cultural Management Consulting, Transnational Management Associates, and Psychological Consultancy Limited.

Getting into the habit of gaining continual, honest feedback from the real world of your customers and your team is a powerful tool.

But there is a subtler challenge when dealing with someone who may appear to be of identical background. The probability is that he or she has very different internal voices and competing commitments.

Dealing with time pressures

No one in a leadership role finds it easy; no one has time to spare. Pressure has increased in recent years from growing competition; greater disclosure requirements and faster returns demanded by shareholders; and for some executives there is criticism from pressure groups, politicians and journalists. How can one attend to something as self-indulgent as personal development when there is so much to do?

We have made the point that personal development is not something separate from the strategy or the task; it is part of making both the setting and execution of strategy more effective. Here we will look at the practical implications for managing the time pressures. Perhaps 'time management' is the wrong term here. One can't do anything about the passage of time; and one can do little about the range of demands placed on us – assuming we attend to such important matters as being assertive (in a courteous fashion) in dealing with those who make the demands. So, if we accept that the passage of time is inexorable and, notwithstanding Albert Einstein's discoveries, can be taken to be constant in our daily experience, and we have established a robust and respectful relationship with the boss or the shareholders, how can we diminish the workload or make it more bearable?

The key lies in equipping ourselves to cope, rather than trying to manage things that we can't control. We can't change what customers want, what technologists invent, what the competition is doing, what shareholders insist on, or what the world price of oil is. But we can make sure that our preparation and attitude are right for leadership. This involves looking after oneself physically and spiritually, in addition to developing the skills that we outline in this book. Tempting as it is to seek outlets in drink and drugs, they tend only to alleviate stress in the short term. Don't worry: this is not a puritanical tract, but a reminder that the term 'work–life balance' includes the concept of *balance*. It's better to let ourselves go after the completion of a project or on holiday. Similarly with working hours: we feel virtuous in working a 14-hour day; but what is the quality of work during that time, and how does it help us deal with tomorrow? We have to look after ourselves.

Tempting as it is to seek outlets in drink and drugs, they tend only to alleviate stress in the short term.

To borrow from the world of sport or music – where continuous coaching and learning are more accepted – we would be shocked at a musician or sports star working for 12 hours the day before a major performance, and then drinking a couple of bottles of wine in the evening. So why do we approach a board meeting in such a casual manner?

Barbara Moorhouse is former finance director of the technology company Kewill Systems. She worked very long hours, involving much transatlantic travel, in periods during the economic downturn, when the company had undergone tough trading conditions and falls in the share price. But she always ensured that she looked after herself through exercise and relaxation – and that she allowed some time for recovery after particularly demanding times.

She comments:

'Coaching helped me understand just how important the management of stress is in business. Since I first started a coaching programme several years ago, I had a brief spell outside of a full-time role and I learned the value of time for myself, and the importance of eating well. Since I began working full-time again that sense of balance has never left me. I make the time to eat properly; I don't drink half a bottle of wine if I can't handle it and I exercise every day. Personal self-management is the foundation for everything; it is not a question of more leisure time. Feeling better about yourself helps you to carry the organization and the people around you.

'This discipline gives you a platform to cope with working in a stressful environment. Then, when you have finished an intensive period of work, you can change the pace. When I come to the end of an intense period I try to create some recovery time. I have just had 16 very intense weeks – I have been in my base country just three of those weeks. I have been involved in projects which are so important to the business that the idea that you can prioritize is nonsense; sometimes you can't do that in business, however good you are at prioritizing. There is too much to do and things come together that can't be delegated or prioritized.

'Everyone I interact with will know if I haven't been looking after myself. They will notice the difference in behaviour on a Monday morning. If you don't look after yourself in a senior role, you are not operating as effectively as you can. But this matters, because there is so much expected of you. None of us can maintain best examples of behaviour if we are continually exhausted.'

Get a coach? Some notes and warnings

Coaching has taken off in recent years. According to a UK survey published in March 2002 by the Industrial Society (now known as the Work Foundation), six out of ten responding organizations offered coaching for senior executives. This rose to eight out of ten large organizations – defined as those employing more than 2,500. Yet the survey indicated that much of the activity is unmonitored. In common with most training and development initiatives, it is done with the aim of boosting individual and team performance but there is little formal evaluation. Fewer than one-third of respondents had an evaluation process.[27]

We are seeking here to tie in assessment, feedback, development and the measurement of performance with the aim of creating a programme of continuous development.

There are pitfalls with coaching, for example, which monitoring would pick up. For example, if the team is under-resourced and is working long hours, this may be the primary cause of performance problems. Coaching the executive misses the main problem, and people may feel resentful at the boss having extra personal attention. This highlights the importance of feedback from the managers and others reporting directly to you. The information received from the direct reports may not directly cite an underlying problem, but any sharp discrepancy between your evaluation of your self and the team's provides the starting point for a discussion. Moreover, if the feedback is done consistently, you can monitor the impact of coaching by examining the change in climate since its start.

David Webster, who co-ordinated the Work Foundation survey, comments:

'Organizations using coaching are hoping to improve individual and company performance and support personal development. These are creditable objectives. But if there isn't an evaluation structure in place for your coaching initiative, how do you know if it is generating success, stagnation or even problems?'

The lack of evaluation of coaching is linked with the attitude we discussed in Chapter 1 – the view that management and leadership are not really learnable skills. If we see our role as being learnable, and one that requires continual development, it follows naturally that we should monitor progress and check whether an initiative has been of any help or not. We'll explore the matter of evaluating and measuring your development further in Chapter 7.

Another potential problem is highlighted by Ian Carlisle, managing director of Autoglass (see Chapter 2 for his case study). He has had a coach for six years, but stresses the importance of having a strong coaching element between boss and subordinate as well (see page 49). There is a danger that the boss can arrange a coach for someone and neglect their own responsibilities for managing the individual. Ian comments:

'I had two coaches: in the business – that is absolutely critical. Having an executive coach is not an abdication for the leader. In too many cases it is seen that way. But to maximize the effectiveness of coaching, your line manager has to be a good coach as well.

'The thing that coaching does is give you external objectivity. No matter how good your boss is in coaching and supporting your development, someone from outside the business can ask more searching questions, and you will be liable to be more honest, because you haven't got the normal boss–subordinate relationship.'

There are some searching questions to ask of the new enthusiasm for coaching that most companies are exhibiting:

◆ Is it covering up dysfunctional team arrangements – for example too many or too few managers?

◆ Is it covering up long working hours and excessive demands on the executive?

◆ Is any evaluation carried out?

◆ Is the coach experienced and qualified?

◆ Is the coach causing the line manager to neglect his or her own coaching responsibilities?

Having said this, the potential of coaching is considerable. The mere act of being considered important enough to be assigned an individual to help with personal performance can boost confidence, and help overcome some of the feelings of isolation that a senior executive can experience, as we discussed in Chapter 1.

Ian Carlisle, who had moved from a structured environment at Marks & Spencer to a role with more autonomy at Autoglass, where he had a coach, adds:

'At Marks & Spencer I was more of a generalist, and strategy just evolved. Here, if you wanted to make something happen you have to make it happen yourself. You have to connect the "how" to the "what". You have to think of implementation. Coaching became very important.

'The other big piece of development was in presentational skills. At Marks & Spencer you rarely went out and presented to people, to the shop floor. Here, in the restructuring, the next challenge was communicating the strategy, how to present, when I had never presented before. I was on stage in front of 250 people. It was my first conference; I organized it. The issue for me was not about what to do, because I knew that. What I wanted was guidance on how to do it. I didn't know how to articulate it in the way that I wanted to. I wanted to inspire people.

'I did some preparation with my coach. She said: "Don't tell them everything. What are the big issues – the ones where you need their support?" She encouraged me and supported me in learning the presentational skills. For advice on presentation I also used people in the company who are good at it. We did rehearsals. Coaching gives you confidence to talk about yourself more than you would. No one's perfect; sharing some of your deficiencies is a strength.'

The restructuring Ian brought about in his previous role as operations director led to a 2 per cent increase in return on sales per year over two years in a mature market. The rehearsals, coaching and preparation he undertook before explaining the strategy to the staff were crucial in making the plans work, he says.

The following examples also illustrate the power of coaching.

Benefits of coaching: Sarah

When Sarah realized that the e-business division she had so successfully started up in 1989 at a large manufacturing conglomerate was going nowhere in terms of the overall business strategy, she turned to the chairman and director of HR to ensure that she would find another job within the company. She had a strong background in finance and had made her way to the top via finance, but had decided that she wanted a more generalist role to enhance her career. She appeared to be well regarded within the company and was offered chief finance officer roles which were seemingly attractive. However, it was not what she wanted. She became extremely agitated that no one was giving her the job she wanted, despite their promises that she would be looked after. 'Trust us,' they said. What she was doing was desperately clinging on to one company and waiting for her company to do something for her. At the age of 35, despite recognizing that the economy was fragile, she had not even thought of actively marketing herself within the company or looking outside of the company for another job.

Complete leaders are constantly benchmarking and updating their skills, not only responding to change, but anticipating it.

She had devoted herself to her job over the last five years, had stood still in terms of her own learning, and was not ready to re-invent herself to keep pace with change. For complete leaders this means staying knowledgeable about market trends and understanding the skills and behaviours that businesses will need down the road. It means being aware of one's own skills and behaviours – of one's strengths and weaknesses – and having a long-term aim to enhance long-term career plans and of course continuing employability. Complete leaders are constantly benchmarking and updating their skills, not only responding to change, but anticipating it.

Through coaching, Sarah began to realize that she needed to reframe some of her values and attitudes. She needed to let go of her traditional view of loyalty: her's to the company and the company's to her. She was shocked to acknowledge that she had to change her view of her career path, which she realized she had taken from her parents; and learn that sticking to one company en route to the top was not necessarily the way forward. She began to understand that her perception of the company as betraying her good faith and excellent performance was not helpful to her, and certainly that getting a reputation for being a 'whiner' would not get her another job. To her surprise she found she lacked some of the skills for getting another job. She also worked through her anger, became more independent-thinking about her career and learnt to get in control of her life again.

She worked through an in-depth self-assessment process, taking stock of those attributes that would influence her effectiveness, success and happiness. She began to understand what interests ignited her, which environments would let her shine, and the skills and behaviours that would help her excel.

Sarah realized that she should stop being so directive with others, and that she needed to learn to be more responsive. Typically she often hadn't bothered to respond to her many e-mails and voicemails, but she hadn't realized how that upset others. She began to listen to the ideas and feelings of others in a more attentive manner, and found that she began to connect better with others. Headhunters too responded more positively to a style that was more empathic and less bossy. This enabled her not only to begin to use her networks, but also to understand what was going on in the market place. She now knew that she wanted to work in a company that was less traditional and bureaucratic, more interested in innovation and change, and where she could be more creative.

Importantly she began to understand how her management style affected others, and how she could function with maximum effectiveness. Armed with a better knowledge of herself, she was able to market herself more effectively, both within the organization as well as with headhunters. Unfortunately, she had neglected her networks outside her company, and she still struggled to meet key people in other businesses.

What she had learnt was to replace her traditional parent–child relationship with the company, and to operate in an adult–adult way. She recognized that she had also dropped her traditional 'blame them' attitude, and felt really empowered to choose the job she wanted. She finally decided to take a CEO job in a turnaround situation within the company. This enabled her to take her family back to Hong Kong for a while, build experience in running an international business in a multicultural environment, and to change her profile from what was perceived as a finance executive to that of a CEO.

She also knew that to remain a complete leader, she need to continuously ask herself the following questions:

◆ Do you actively seek out new learning opportunities at work, things that would enhance your value to the organization, thus broadening your professional knowledge?

◆ Are you paying enough attention to office politics, relationships and communication, or are you still focusing too much of your time on tasks and balance sheets? Are you staying well connected to others?

◆ Are you building your professional network to draw on for advice, support, and job leads?

◆ Are you beginning to work on the job after next, and where you want to be when you are 40 (or 50 or 60)?

◆ Are you continuing to grow, change and learn?

chapter seven
measuring your progress

Learning points from this chapter

◆ There is not a good reason for *not* checking your effectiveness.

◆ Precise measures on many aspects of leadership are not possible; but it is still better to have some indicators.

◆ The measures are straightforward; give graphic indication of relative progress, and can be incorporated into continual communication and team development.

◆ External measures of technical skills of team members can be useful as a team building exercise.

How can you measure leadership performance? Why should you do it?

Let's explore the second question first. It may seem illogical to attempt precise measures of an intangible matter such as the diverse, complex and subtle skills of a modern business leader.

We invert the onus. Your personal development is integral to your success and that of your organization. It should not be done in an amateurish or 'cross-fingers-and-hope' manner. There is not a good reason for *not* checking whether the sometimes expensive and time-consuming interventions are having a positive effect.

Organizations have traditionally not measured whether the return they obtain from their investments in training and development of managers (or anyone else, for that matter) is worthwhile. This is not a sustainable attitude. The vast bulk of the assets of a modern organization are its people, networks, skills, intellectual networks and organizational knowledge. The bulk of its meaningful investment will be on people. It is not logical for this to be made in an unplanned way.

Spending on the personal development of leaders can be considerable. Some form of measures, both collective and individual, will be needed. On personal development, we can't pretend that we can put precise figures to everything; the point is to have a reliable, relative measure of progress, by keeping the evaluation process consistent. This leads us on to the 'how'.

The process that we have explored of developing self-awareness by comparing your perception of yourself with how you come across to others, is not a one-off. Development is a continual process.

There is little point in going through this process unless you have improved; and you need to find out if you have improved. So you can repeat the questionnaires (pages 69 and 71) after, say, six months or a year – and see if the scores you give yourself are closer to those your team give you, and whether you have improved on a key style that required improvement, be it the authoritative or the democratic style.

This is a relative, subjective measure, but it is perfectly valid, because it's the relative, subjective experience of your leadership that determines the motivation of your team or organization, which in turn determines whether your customers buy from you. It's the measure that matters. So if you had rated yourself as eight out of ten on the democratic style, but were only given three out of ten by your employees, a good measure is whether the employee rating had improved after your commitment to involve them more in decisions.

Feedback: some notes on how to engender continual, two-way feedback with your team

If you're not used to asking your staff for honest feedback on how you come across to them and how you lead, it can be difficult to get started. Of course, 360-degree appraisals have been fashionable in many corporate circles, but not in all organizations, and there have been question marks about how reliable the information is from such exercises in organizations where trust isn't very high. It has been documented that requesting such comprehensive, detailed feedback on managers can be counterproductive in organizations not accustomed to performance reviews, or where staff are insecure and therefore have little incentive to be honest. From the individual manager's point of view, the thought of uncensored comments from direct reports can be 'scary', even in seasoned and mature individuals, particularly where there have been organizational dysfunctions:

If you're not used to asking your staff for honest feedback on how you come across to them and how you lead, it can be difficult to get started.

'As with any management tool, 360-degree appraisal depends upon commitment and upon an atmosphere that is supportive. Poor morale at the outset or poor implementation can lead to the use of this valuable tool as a weapon. If an organization is in trauma then the immediate causes must be dealt with before trying to use a sophisticated process that depends for its success upon commitment . . . 360-degree appraisal is also better suited to an organization where performance appraisal is already in operation and people are accustomed to the idea of having their performance assessed. The change arising from introducing both notions at once can be too much of a shock to some staff, giving rise to levels of suspicion and hostility that can be hard to deal with successfully. Sometimes people find the idea of 360-degree appraisal threatening and imagine that they are going to be told about everything that is wrong with them.'[28]

These observations apply directly to the 360-degree process, in which feedback is gathered from colleagues, superiors, direct reports and customers in a systematic way, generally with the help of questionnaires. Obviously, however, the same general principles and cautions apply to any structured form of securing feedback.

Nonetheless, such words of advice highlight the importance of establishing the groundwork for feedback to be obtained; it doesn't detract from the power and usefulness of gaining that information when this is done in a conscientious manner. In this book we argue that to become a fully complete leader, an accurate perception of how you lead at the moment is essential. Irrespective of whether your organization has a formal means of gaining feedback, it's useful to develop the habit of gaining at least some impression of how you come across to others. Obviously, it would be irritating and confusing for a team if you were to be overly self-conscious and forever asking, 'How did I come across in that presentation?' Your team needs leadership and it is a mistake to be too open about feelings and insecurities, as we'll discuss again in the remaining chapters. The trick is to try to gain a picture of ourselves. In an earlier chapter we introduced the metaphor of waiting for a photograph to come back from the developers. We may believe we were perfectly groomed as we posed for the photographer, but what will the prints reveal?

There are even ways of gaining a picture of what our team thinks of us without asking them. A trusted PA, for example, can be invaluable. The day after a tricky presentation to the team, you can ask her (or him), 'Did that go down well? What are their worries? Did I allay them? What are they looking for?' Your PA is likely to be a trusted confidante, and able to be honest without jeopardizing her relationship either with you or with the team.

Claire Hall-Moore, an associate partner at consultancy group Accenture, comments:

'I have asked my direct reports for feedback. Accenture places a lot of emphasis on leadership development and we have introduced a leadership self-analysis process that I used to structure the feedback. One real surprise was that some junior staff perceptions were very focused on my job title and how that puts me in a position of power. This can make me, or my role seem remote to their daily job. That was a surprise to me, because I did not see myself as being different to the person I was a couple of years ago (before my promotion). But clearly because of the change in job title you can be seen as being somehow different. It is something that I have to keep in mind so that my team feel that I am approachable.

'One real surprise was that some junior staff perceptions were very focused on my job title and how that puts me in a position of power.'

'Amongst the positive feedback was the fact that my direct reports really did value the support that I give them. They saw me as stretching them; they saw me as having a very strong "can do" approach, which rubs off on the team in terms of them saying "we can do this." It was really useful to understand what I do to generate this view.'

Through coaching, Claire assessed herself on how well she rated on three core motives: affiliation, power and achievement. She rated strongly on all, but especially on achievement (task focus). This helped her appreciate her own strengths, and recognize that those of other people might be quite different. One-to-one sessions with her members of staff, combined with the coaching process, helped enormously in building up this picture and better enable her to deploy the talents her team has.

She comments also on how the combination of formal and informal feedback, getting to know your team, and learning how to handle people, leads to continual improvement in both self-awareness and awareness of others. This has a direct effect on business performance:

'It is important to demonstrate to your team that they can do something. If you can give them feedback about how they thought a project was going to be really hard but they achieved successful outcomes anyway and get them to think about why, then you can get them to build on this and do more. You can give them confidence, and relating this to their work makes this tangible. Knowing them helps. Being patient helps. Patience is not my biggest strength – I do get very focused on getting the job done – so I have to remember to pace myself and remember that there is always an optimum speed.

'When I get very focused on getting the job done I also need to make sure that my communication skills are up to speed. I need to stop and explain what I want up front and not go with my first reaction which is to dive in and get the job done. That is where I have learned to be more patient. If you say, "Just do it," you risk getting the wrong result.'

Market rating an executive as part of a development programme

An external measure of effectiveness can be used effectively also. In the example below, we will see how one firm instituted a development programme for a team, the results of which were higher performance, less time lost in conflicts, and better retention. A key feature was to incorporate a way of measuring the effectiveness of the members. A personnel executive involved in the process takes up the story:

'We decided to create a shared service centre. This brought together five or six different businesses that did not have a shared sense of identity or a shared way of doing business. My contribution to creating this identity was getting the executive team to work together. They were all strong individuals who had never worked together before as a team. They were high achievers and they enjoyed the achievement of running their bit of the business – in a way being "mini-CEOs".

'I designed a programme of team-building and individual coaching for each of the executive team members, including me. When I took the job on some of the very senior leaders in the firm told me that I had to make this team work better, otherwise we would not succeed.

'We used a search and selection agency to give us a market assessment of each of these senior individuals at the beginning of this team-building. We were able to say: "Here is an objective assessment about you; how you measure up against other purchasing directors or marketing directors." All of them were rated strongly compared with their peers so we started this process with them knowing that they were not under threat as individuals.

'The real test came fairly recently, when we had to disband the team [because of a reorganization] after two years of building up loyalty, interdependence and personal trust. A managing director role was created and three of our executive team were candidates. We decided our appointment would be internal. The worry was that we would lose the two unsuccessful candidates.

'Both of those individuals are still with the company. In one case he said he was going to leave, and got to the point of leaving when we persuaded him to stay. I said, "You can do other great things here." I said that knowing his history and knowing him well; this had come out of that executive team-building, so I knew him and could have that conversation; and he had got to know himself. The other candidate said, "That's OK; I accept the decision. I thought I could have done a better job but I will work for you." Anyone who knew him two years ago would not have believed that he would have been like that – he used to be very volatile and has worked on that. Then he was offered another opportunity within the firm.'

chapter eight

you are on stage but not acting – an awareness of the public nature of the leader's role

Learning points from this chapter

- Development is a process, not an event.

- The team grows through continual feedback.

- Never underestimate the motivational power of praise for an employee.

- Learning presentational skills aids leadership development.

Everyone has had the experience of being wonderfully inspired at a training event, then returned to work confident that 'everything will be different', only to find that the familiar pressures, distractions and frustrations reappear with alacrity. By the morning of the second day back it feels that 'nothing is different' but for a vaguely positive emotion associated with communicating with others on the away-day or training course.

Training, or self-development, is often conceived of as being an event with a goal rather than as an ongoing process. We can be lulled into thinking that we have 'done' this or that bit of development, such as how to manage a project or motivate a staff member. In reality personal development is a daily discipline, ideally with built-in forms of feedback and some measures to test your improvement.

In reality personal development is a daily discipline, ideally with built-in forms of feedback and some measures to test your improvement.

The task of charting your ability, and mapping the perception of you that your team has, will have given you immense potential to improve your performance and that of your team. This has to be sustained. After all, the very best musicians or sports stars carry on training even when they are at the top. Complete leadership requires the same. This might seem daunting, but because it leads to better communication, management and performance, it is naturally self-sustaining.

Take the observation of Claire Hall-Moore, associate partner at Accenture:

'My coaching began about a year ago. Initially I had some doubts about how much I was going to get from it. I have spent a large part of my career very focused on other people's development – my background is organizational development, which has taken me into the area of personal and leadership development. I suppose I had an unconscious assumption that all of that work with other people had probably rubbed off on me and that consequently I had some doubts about how far I would get with coaching; I felt I was quite self-aware already and wondered whether there could be any truly new revelations.

'But my coach [Susan Bloch] was able to reflect back immediately how I was coming across – there is something to do with timing here. She would say, "This is what you have just said; this is how you came across. Why did you go down that particular avenue?" That really helped me sharpen up my self-awareness and learn from what I was doing. This ties in to the team-based approach [at Accenture]. There is always someone to learn more from. I would hate to think that there was nothing more to learn.'

As we discussed in Chapter 2 (see page 39), we can move towards the subjects of our conversations and aspirations, but this is a gradual process, not a magical transformation.

Claire Hall-Moore adds:

'With development you need to take on board aspects and elements that fit with you. You can't turn yourself into someone else. Incremental development is likely to fit more appropriately; you are not going to suddenly change into a different person. As you take small steps you can take stock and adjust what you are doing.'

The team grows as well

In Chapter 5 we noted that while leadership involves authority and direction, it is not a solo or dictatorial discipline. It is both rational and emotional, and it engages with the collective. Delivery of targets, services or deadlines is important, but so are ideas; and delivery is more likely to be efficient and on time if those in the team responsible feel that they are able to contribute ideas, that they own the processes and are highly motivated to give of their best.

In this chapter we will emphasize and explore how the leader and team can grow and develop together.

Continual feedback is an essential part of this. It also needs to be two-way: you need to know how you are coming across, and those in your team need to know how they are doing. One of the most extraordinary aspects about leadership is how seldom some managers simply say 'thank you' or 'well done' to a staff member doing an exceptional job, especially if combined with enthusiastic, specific praise, such as, 'I think you have a real gift for chairing a meeting and defusing problems.' Probably nothing we do is more motivational; few things are more profitable for the company; it costs nothing, takes little time, yet we rarely do it. Most people want to feel good about themselves, and they will walk through fire for a leader who thinks they are a genius. We often expect our colleagues and direct reports to work until late into the evening to meet deadlines; to sacrifice some of the personal time to meet a team's goal, and sometimes simply forget to thank them or inform them, quite factually, that they are doing a complex, challenging job with a high degree of skill and integrity.

Most people want to feel good about themselves, and they will walk through fire for a leader who thinks they are a genius.

So having learned the value of feedback, the importance of it being two-way, it is timely to ask yourself a few months after starting the process, 'Is it still happening? Was it just a one-off?'

Andy Parfitt: 'I discovered I was presenting all the time'

In Chapter 2, we emphasized that complete leadership is about letting all your abilities shine; that development is about building on your personality, not suppressing it to conform to a managerial archetype. The experience of Andy Parfitt, controller of BBC Radio 1 in the UK, gives a vivid illustration of this. It finds its way into this chapter as an example of someone who has gone through much of the learning that we have described, and whose team is now growing with his development, and how this development is built on his innate abilities and personality.

When Andy took over in 1998, Radio 1 was struggling to maintain itself as the premier station for young listeners. The BBC is an institution with a long history and august reputation, in which a station aimed primarily at young people that may feature controversial acts like Eminem or Marilyn Manson, sometimes sits a little uneasily. Moreover, competition had grown exponentially in the 1980s and 1990s, with dozens of commercial music stations being set up. The BBC is in the highly unusual position of being funded by a ring-fenced tax, being accountable to politicians and required to uphold its principles of impartiality and fairness, but also expected to be thoroughly competitive, including with the youth market. Andy's role is very much in the public eye, and some of his staff are nationally known personalities with formidable egos and a massive fan base. Any personnel difficulties he has are likely to be splashed across the popular papers as well as the business pages.

The weight of the history of the organization, and of the responsibilities he faced, caused him to be anxious in his early days, and to suppress his personal instincts. Moreover, the corporation in the 1990s had instilled many managerial controls that had been lacking earlier. While this improved financial control and accountability, there had been a tendency to put too much emphasis on management and to stifle creativity, according to many who worked in the organization. Andy now takes up the story:

'I knew in the back of my mind that my personal development and confidence was going to be really important, but at the time I was at the beginning of that journey. So although I knew that it was important, I think that the prospect of the job meant that I underplayed it, because I wasn't confident that I could use my own personality. I underplayed the fact that I was now important.

'Probably I feel now that I'm aware that everything you do is a major signal: the clothes you wear; the events you attend; the things you don't attend; or how you react to news, for example, about a competitor. The signals you send are very loud if you are controller. An early lesson for me was that if you don't understand your importance you can send a lot of conflicting messages, or ones not befitting a leader.

'When I first became controller, because my own assessment of my own performance was about audience ratings – not to an overwhelming extent but there was an issue about ratings, a feeling that they were not as robust as they might be – I quite unconsciously put the focus in team meetings on ratings performance. I started to give out the message that it was all about ratings. I just became overly reliant on concrete measures of success, and measurement and performance began to dominate forums where the accent should have been on the product and the people making the contribution; celebrating successes and reviewing in a positive way.

'You only have a limited amount of quality time talking to all of your team, so if you unconsciously fill that quality time with the wrong sort of stuff it's not only a waste of that time but it puts a skew on what people perceive to be the overall objective of the organization. That did happen at first and it is less motivating, because individual people couldn't see the connection with their own endeavours, enthusiasms and skills, and the impact on this very bald quarterly figure that comes through called a rating. That is demoralizing; there is pressure to perform but without knowing where the levers are.

'I now think that listening to your own core team; being relaxed enough in the role to be able to listen and think about what might fill those quality moments is the priority.

'There was a "light bulb" moment. When I started I used to be a nervy public speaker. I felt the weight of the organizational history on my shoulders if faced with the responsibility of representing the BBC. It held me back from using my personality. It is short-hand and glib, but you have to learn to be yourself at work to be most effective. Someone I worked with gave me some honest feedback. He said: "Why do you change from being passionate, articulate and funny when speaking in public and become an automaton?" It was searing feedback. I think that one of my strengths is that I am a self-starter and a self-improver. If someone says something potentially useful then I take note. I didn't have much in the way of formal education but I have been a self-improver. I could see that I could learn, and I am very good at sourcing a person who could help me. I remember going on the recommendation of someone else to do presentation training.

'As it turned out, the individual didn't just help me with presentation, but with giving me the courage of my convictions and showing me that being myself is enough. After a few sessions I was captured with the idea; that I was at my best when being me.

'How can you be fully creative if you don't use your full personality? The Andy that plays guitar, paints, has two daughters and was in three bands. You shouldn't leave that behind. This was linked to the matter of being able to show my weaknesses. It's incredibly powerful for others; they realize that this is not one of those managers that we have all worked with who feel they know how to do everything and are brilliant – they are demoralizing to work for. You feel you can make a contribution if someone has said, "I can't do this." To have the guts to say, "Here I am; here's my response as Andy Parfitt." Then, when you make the discovery that everyone in these leadership positions has experiences and concerns it becomes a relief.

'The things that I learned on the presentation course concerned matters such as relaxation; eye contact; personability; use of voice; pausing; the feeling that I could throw the light on a member of staff and give them praise. When you are more self-concious all those things go, it's all about you, not all about them as it should be. I also learned little techniques to challenge people whose behaviour in meetings is disruptive.

'I also realized – and this is how the impact of the training went way beyond public speaking ability – that as a leader you are presenting all the time, in the sense of managing your personality. You are presenting when you talk to a direct report; you are presenting when you talk to your boss – and everyone has a boss.

'I used to take notes [during the presentation training]. Every time I had to give a speech I would go through my notes; I tried to bring them alive for myself again. I had to give a speech about young people at the Labour Party conference, and Prime Minister Tony Blair was in the audience, as well as the deputy chair of the BBC governors, plus 300 party people. I remember thinking that the best I could achieve was just get through it, with Mr Blair being such a consummate public speaker himself. It passed well and I got some positive responses.

'The trouble with nervousness and stage fright is that it shuts you down. You can't listen; you can't relax. Nerves close people's personalities down and you become wooden.

'Now in the office, and when I address the staff, the atmosphere is conducive for people to be honest. People ask more questions. The main thing is that meetings are fun. There is laughter, with people spontaneously applauding others for their contributions. There is positiveness and ease; it is a different situation. Instead of putting something in writing on a screen [when addressing the staff], I would rather have a big image on the screen, like a picture of Mary J. Blige when talking about RnB, instead of a list of bullet points.

'There is stuff outside your control; but you can't get het up about it. I can't know everything that's going on at Capital Radio [the main competitor to Radio 1 in London]. If you worry about the bottom line then you're not concentrating on the product or the people. If you think about people, the rest takes care of itself. I do more and more talking about people and how to motivate them.

'That is my job: to make it a really great place to work. If you ask most young radio presenters where they aspire to work they still say Radio 1.'

There is an interesting dynamic here: by not focusing on the bottom line, the bottom line improves. This is not the paradox it appears to be, when we remind ourselves, as noted in Chapter 2, that measurable results are simply the end result of what people do. If you set desired results as targets it doesn't work, but motivate people to deliver and you will achieve what you want and more. By early 2001/2 Radio 1 had restored its reputation as the premier pop station in the UK. In the third quarter of 2001 it achieved a record reach of 57 per cent of 15–24-year-olds; the website had 4 million page impressions, and in 2001 around 750,000 people attended Radio 1 live events. Andy Parfitt still finds time to play guitar.

By not focusing on the bottom line, the bottom line improves.

Barbara Moorhouse: on stage but not acting

Andy Parfitt's example above illustrates how complete leadership is about letting your personality and qualities shine, but in a leadership way, with a clear sense of purpose for the organization as well as for yourself. There is a balance to be struck here, or rather a combination to be sought – letting your personality shine does not mean being self-indulgent. It means developing those abilities you possess that aid the team, the situation and the company.

Being a leader means setting a vision, but not indulging in fantasy. It means being on stage; but you are not acting. (See also the discussion on authoritative leadership on page 47.)

This implies being aware that you are being watched and that your behaviour and performance matter. Andy Parfitt benefited from tailored coaching on how to speak in public. Another executive, Barbara Moorhouse, former finance director at the UK-based firm Kewill Systems, had a similar epiphany. In a previous role, which she describes as having 'a boring title' but being a fascinating job, she was director of regulation at a utility company South West Water in the UK. It involved a considerable amount of media work. The industry had recently been privatized; there was controversy over the possible introduction of meters for water use, and a couple of years earlier there had been a serious poisoning of the water supply at a town called Camelford in the region, which was found to have been due to negligence by the water company.

Barbara recalls being hissed at when addressing the Women's Institute (a venerable national institution in Britain) – a fate that was even to befall Prime Minister Tony Blair a few years later. She recalls:

'It was a major regional conference of theirs in Cornwall. As I walked to the platform they hissed. Being female didn't save me. But I am pleased to say that after the presentation I was applauded roundly. Afterwards some of them said that they hadn't understood the matters from the company's perspective before. That anecdote shows at least one thing: how I have learned to understand other people's viewpoint. If they feel very strongly, there is probably a reason. You may not agree, but understanding is actually quite important.

'This is important in my current job, where I go to many functions, which are sometimes intimidating; sometimes I wonder, "What am I doing here?" But I remember that every person has their story. If you keep talking then you'll find something that's on their wavelength. It comes back to remembering that management is a human process and you are dealing with people. Some people get hung up on the status, the mechanics and the task issues – I know that I used to.'

Skills, once acquired, don't stay within the categories that we assign to our different areas of responsibility.

Like Andy Parfitt, her rapid learning in public speaking had benefits far beyond that of giving an effective speech. Skills, once acquired, don't stay within the categories that we assign to our different areas of responsibility. Communication is a key part of becoming a complete leader and the abilities deployed for a public audience can be used also for an internal one. Moreover, its benefits are two-way: not only has Barbara increased her ability to convey a message, but also to understand the views of other constituencies – for example, by being confronted very publicly with the dissenting views of Women's Institute members. She continues:

'When I came to the job as finance director it was the end of March [financial year-end in the UK]. We had to give preliminary results in June, and announce an acquisition. My predecessor had stayed on for the handover and we were going to give the results together. At the last minute he left a voicemail saying that he couldn't get back from the States in time and could I do it. I got through it. I had done so much press and PR work at South West Water, and, with the coaching on top, that's a very powerful combination. You go into role and you almost strip out the internal uncertainties.

'But although I think of it as a stage I am not acting. You have to have integrity. You are being yourself but it is that part of yourself that the company needs at that time. It's about finding a way to be positive – being positive, not just thinking positive.

'For example, my staying positive and optimistic during difficult trading conditions has been crucially important. People look me in the eyes and ask: "Are we going to come through?" If my behaviour flickers even for a moment I'm going to have mass resignations. This is not acting; more fundamentally you have to find a way to believe. If internally you are doubtful, then people will pick it up. What you have to do is say: "I am going to see and articulate a way forward." It may not be successful, but what you can give people is a sense of purpose; a sense of constructive momentum and a sense of personal interest in what they do and acknowledge that the business will face risks, but you try to give a sense that "we can do this." Anyone has a choice: I will set a direction.

'If I left the business I would hope that my perspective on its prospects would be unaffected. Fundamentally it's about integrity; finding a positive, rather than pretending there is one.

'PR training was about how to be in front of the camera, and to leave your insecurities and doubts off-camera. Coaching enabled me to do that not just in front of the camera but to imagine that all the time you are working on stage; in the same way as if there *was* a camera. The only difference is that the word 'stage' implies acting, and people pick it up if you are insincere. As people we are all incredibly good behavioural sleuths; we pick it up. You are yourself; but conscious of being in front of people who are looking at you. It's a case of trying to take your own best; the things that you can be – not trying to be someone you're not.'

All her media and public speaking training and experience have had a direct benefit on how Barbara performs as a senior executive. Like Andy Parfitt, she finds that she is presenting all the time.

chapter nine
did I just get better?
complete leadership in
action

Learning points from this chapter

- Everyone has a boss; how to manage the boss is part of being a leader.

- Sometimes it's better to show, rather than tell.

- A tactical silence can say much.

- Other people's anger is their problem.

At this stage in your development, you will have a good awareness of your strengths and weaknesses; and so will your team. You will have embarked on a plan of developing the strengths such that you can deploy the range of managerial styles we have set out, and relate to people in an emotionally mature manner.

Here we give some examples of complete leadership in action, taking two of the most tricky situations executives face: managing their boss, and dealing with collective negotiations.

How to manage your boss

Everyone has a boss. The boss is not always the leader.

These two counter-intuitive statements are worth bearing in mind during this chapter; and indeed during your development as a leader. The first of these is not obvious, but merits some reflection.

The CEO has investors; the investors have investors. The analysts have bosses; board members can be sacked. Presidents and prime ministers can be voted out. Everyone is in some way accountable, and no one has the absolute guarantee of a job for life. There is always someone looking at your performance and judging whether it comes up to scratch. There is always someone with the authority to tell you what to do, if only on occasion and under certain circumstances.

Understanding and managing your boss provides you with a pleasant work environment and you and the business become much more effective. To do this, you need to gain a good understanding of both your boss and yourself, especially with regard to management styles, learning styles, strengths and weaknesses. It's important to clarify mutual expectations and agree how you are going to work together effectively. Think about how your boss likes to receive information or communication. Is it by e-mail, phone or voicemail? Or only by face to face meetings? Don't assume, just because *you* don't like receiving calls on your mobile phone while you're on holiday that your boss feels the same.

Understanding and managing your boss provides you with a pleasant work environment and you and the business become much more effective.

Terry, the MD of a large fast-moving consumer-goods business in Europe and who is based in Paris, received feedback that his boss John, based in Chicago, did not trust him. Terry rarely initiated any form of communication with his boss, and was surprised to see how, by sending John regular e-mails of updates on sales, their relationship became transformed. As John felt he was no longer cut out of important communication, he became more relaxed and did not dig for detail in the manner that Terry had found irritating; and was greatly appreciative of the updates he received. This he felt kept him connected with the European business.

Initially, try to understand the pressures on your boss, what his or her organizational and personal goals are, and what he or she needs from you. Be sensitive to his management style and how it is similar or different to yours. Become aware of what it is about you that might help or hinder the way you work with your boss. Then take actions that make the relationship more effective. Avoid being either overly dependent on or independent from your boss, and try to foster collaborative interdependence.

And remember, you will always have a boss even if you are one. At the most senior level our bosses are venture capitalists, bank managers, investors, and even customers.

CORE QUESTIONS TO ASK

◆ How can I make my boss my partner?

◆ What does my boss need from me?

◆ What do I need from my boss?

◆ How can we both benefit from this relationship?

WHAT A BOSS NEEDS FROM YOU

◆ Loyalty

◆ Protection

◆ Career enhancement

◆ Delivery

Managing the boss can be demanding, and is easily overlooked. If neglected, though, we are storing up trouble. As we noted in Chapter 2, it can be easy to forget that management is about relationships and people. We think instead that it's all about targets, goals and processes. Accompanying this self-deception is the common assumption that those 'above us' are not really people with feelings and with weaknesses and that our contact with them doesn't form a relationship that can be worked at. Let's tackle these common and damaging misconceptions.

If, for example, we fail to be sufficiently assertive and the boss is excessively demanding, we place too much pressure on ourselves and on our direct reports. But we can't tell the boss what to do. Can we?

Well, it is true that we can't tell the boss what to do. The coercive style of management is limited even where it is a senior manager managing down the line; it's likely to be even more problematic if we adopt it for managing up. But handling the boss is an essential part of becoming a complete leader; there are times when your immediate superior is wrong, or too demanding, or behaving in a damaging way. You can't scold him or her, but what you can do is deploy your complete leadership skills to limit the damage and coax the individual into a more mature and rational way of behaving, as we'll see now (for obvious reasons, the names have been changed).

Candy's story – how she managed her boss

Candy was the finance director of a firm founded by a colourful character called Dan. She drew on skills developed in coaching to intervene in order to lessen the damage of Dan's outbursts, particularly those with investors. She takes up the story:

'There was a series of investor meetings. Dan is charismatic, but volatile, and he had never learned the technique of not being defensive; he could be in sales, where he was brilliant, but, with investors whom he didn't particularly like, he could be incredibly hostile. At one time we were very highly rated and we had a meeting with 12 managers at a major investment banking firm. It was a big ticket audience.

'Dan would take every form of challenge as a criticism. Occasionally he would actually be horns locked in a row with an investor. I was just thinking "This is a no-no." I had learned both from my coaching and from generally watching what you should do in such situations that this was wrong. Whatever investors do, it is ultimately their company. Whatever they choose to ask, you have a duty to answer courteously, rigorously and accurately. The idea that you should be defensive about what is their business I find astonishing.

'I found myself in the investment round trying to mediate. I made sure that I was always the last one out of the lift, so that I could leave a courteous impression with the people whom we had been meeting. I would say something like, "It's been a long round of meetings," in effect excusing his behaviour.

'I was making excuses for him; trying to maintain the image of the organization, and trying to make sure that I personally established a rapport with investors. I was trying to represent the company, and modify his behaviour in a way that would blunt the more extreme aspects. After one meeting where, in my view, I had successfully mediated, he was clearly angry at the way the meeting had been handled, and said so. I went silent, and this was effective. My instinctive reaction was to respond but, informed partly by my coaching, I thought that I would say nothing. For me it is difficult because I am chatty, but I just absorbed it. Those of us who are quick-thinking, quick-talking and see ourselves as decisive are uncomfortable with inaction, but there is value in staying silent sometimes. You don't always have to say the first thing that comes into your mind. Before coaching if I didn't have an answer it would worry me, and I would feel inadequate. You have to learn not to panic about not knowing what to do.'

Candy's silence at this juncture was not inaction, however. It was a subtle and effective form of feedback, which helped Dan see how he had behaved. Had she shouted back, then her words and emotions would have entered the stage, clouding the issue. When people argue, they respond to the response, not to the underlying problem, which becomes obscured. This moment of silence drew out Dan's poison, and highlighted the fact that that was all there was. Candy was saying, 'This is your problem with managing anger; don't put it onto me.' After this, the two developed a strong rapport and became an effective partnership. The firm managed to maintain investor confidence in difficult global economic conditions.

Complete leadership in negotiations

A similar act of mature management to the one that Candy demonstrated can be seen in the following anecdote from a human resources manager. It takes us into the world of negotiations and brinkmanship. But note how the same skill in handling the combustible boss is used in handling combustible trade unions.

Sandra is an interim manager. As such, she always expects two things. The unexpected and the need to adapt to her circumstances. Her latest assignment was as an industrial relations specialist within a leading international airport. This was a tough environment, male-dominated and entrenched in tradition and one-upmanship. One of the main trade unions quite naturally decided to utilize its strength in order to place pressure on the company during one of the protracted annual pay negotiations. Sandra takes up the story:

'My previous experience with trade unions was essentially nil. The company's recognized trade unions knew this, and decided to play it to their advantage. They were used to dealing with men, with tough negotiators, people they had grown up with, on the opposite side of the bargaining table, for the last 10 to 15 years. A mere whipper-snapper of a woman in her early 30s, new to the industry with no experience of trade unions, was surely the best joker the company had pulled out of their pack of cards in years.

'As an interim manager you are given a tight schedule. Deliver within that timeframe or else. However, that is the flip side. There is no "or else". That is what you are paid to do. To deliver. I had six months from beginning to end and a mass of other projects and negotiations to deliver alongside this particular objective. I wasn't going to let the traditional male-orientated attitudes stand in the company's way of moving the negotiations forward.

'Everything had been progressing smoothly enough – well, as best as it can do when you are dealing with five different trade unions and hence six different points of view including the company's. One thing, however, slowly became evident: the two main unions distrusted one another intensely, and that could only be to my advantage. I didn't know when my opportunity would arise, as the bickering between the two delayed everything to twice the length of time it should have done, but I knew that I had found their weakness.

'All of the individual topics for discussion were mapped out across my calendar, one after the other with very little room for manoeuvre. The unions also had this schedule, and delighted every year in one of their favourite tactics which was to delay the schedule by any means possible until it reached stretching point, so that they could then back the company into a corner just before the formally recognized pay review date.

'The latest session was scheduled for the afternoon, with me kicking off the company's presentation. I had scarely reached slide four before I could sense that there was disquiet within the room. With up to 40 people seated before me, I couldn't sense quite where it came from, but its presence was definitely making itself felt. I continued onto the next slide and decided against opening up to the floor for comments. I told myself to let the audience hear what I had to say and then they could debate it, but at least they could let me have the decency to finish what I had to say. But no. It wasn't going to happen. First one, then another would slowly stand up and without looking at me, walk out of the room.

'My heart fluttered and internally I began to panic. This was not good news. I tried to ignore it, telling myself that they must have received an urgent message on their pagers. In airports, there are always life-and-death emergencies, and if your pager goes off, you don't ignore it. But then that couldn't be it, otherwise the managers representing the company would also have left the room. They must be leaving because the company view was just so disparate and distant from what they expected to hear.

'I took a deep breath, refocused my mind and continued. Barely had I got the words out of my mouth before another one stood up and walked out. Then somewhere in the back of my brain, I struck lucky. I spotted that the man who was now busy sliding out of the door towards his tea and biscuits would not have seen the men who had already escaped, although he would have heard them. The important fact was that he had been sitting in front of them and he hadn't looked around. In fact, all of the representatives from one of the two major trade unions hadn't turned their heads, and yet here they were walking out of the door. It was all the same trade union. The last person had stood up before I had even managed to speak another full sentence, so it wasn't what I was saying that was the problem. It was all planned.

'My first fleeting thoughts had been that their need for tea and biscuits was greater than I could possibly imagine, but no: this was obviously a set-up. And quite a clever one. Without any formal training in how to deal with a situation like this, if something was designed to throw me off balance, this would.

'The obvious question was, "What do I do?" Do I draw attention to the fact by suspending my presentation, leaving the room and asking them to re-enter until the scheduled tea-break? This was clearly not an option I wished to pursue. My instinct told me that this manoeuvre would put me into a position of weakness and them in a position of strength. They would have won. The only other option was to carry on regardless and think of a tactical position as I spoke. Logic, and partly anger, caused me to ask myself, "If they couldn't be bothered to stay to listen to my side of the argument, then how could they fully contribute in the following debate?" The answer was simple. They couldn't.

'However, when I lifted my eyes, what I did have in front of me were four trade unions, one of whom was the main opponent of the union whose representatives were busily but noiselessly departing out through the doors. The representatives of the other unions were still sitting in front of me, and what's more, they were listening. Instead of throwing me off my guard, I could actually use it to my advantage. I finished the scheduled part of my talk, and added onto the end of it, as though planned, that a motion would be voted on at the end of the afternoon regarding the topic in question, and that, as previously agreed prior to negotiations having commenced, the majority vote would count.

'This was news indeed to the remaining main trade union. From previous "off the record" discussions with all of the trade unions, I knew that this union was pretty much in alignment with the company on this particular issue. I also knew that its rival was as far apart from the company as it was possible to be on the matter, and that the union representatives who had stayed would not miss out on the opportunity to score a point over their main rivals.

'In the debate that followed, they certainly weren't slow in raising one or two opportunistic proposals. But, confident in my new status at being able to hand them something on a plate which they hadn't dreamed of during weeks of hard negotiations, I tightened down even more in favour of the company. I knew without doubt that they would vote in favour of the company's proposal at the end of the afternoon, whatever that proposal might be, even if their sole objective was purely to spite their main rival. I could afford to be tough. Just because I had given them a plate, did not mean that I was going to adorn it with meat and vegetables as well. At the end of a very rewarding afternoon's discussion without the usual accusations and comments flying backwards and forth, the motion was carried and quickly documented. The documentation quite naturally made mention to the fact that a certain named trade union had decided not to be present for the whole of the afternoon's discussions, including an important opportunity to vote for or against the company's motion regarding this item.

'This covered my organization's back in case the union's shop stewards at a later date strongly objected to the company's dealings in the matter. "Well," I could quite honestly say, "as you will see from the minutes, your trade union had the opportunity, but they chose not to act upon it."

'Of course in the short term, there was a lot of anger directed my way, like ". . . but you can't do that." My response to which was a simple, "I can and I have. This is the schedule. You knew what the schedule was. You knew what topic was being debated. You know that the majority vote counts. If you had stayed seated for the rest of my presentation, you would have realized that there was, as there have been in all of the major discussions up to now, a motion to be voted on at the end of the debate which becomes automatically integrated into this year's pay negotiations. You had your chance to influence the agreement and the vote but you chose not to take that opportunity. If you don't wish to represent your members' interests, then that's fine. That's your choice."

'Needless to say, they did turn up on time, if not early, on every occasion after that, and strangely enough always stayed through to the end, even if that meant undergoing the fiercest of debates with their main and bitterest rival. On more than one occasion, they harped back to the particular topic that had been under debate that day. And on every occasion they raised it, I told them just as firmly that the topic was no longer open for discussion.

'With the pay negotiations finally complete, my brief was complete, and I could wave goodbye to yet another enjoyable and immensely rewarding interim assignment.'

10

chapter ten
you never stop improving

Learning points from this chapter

◆ It is never a good idea to assume you have arrived and to 'rest on your oars'.

◆ Complete leadership means letting your ability and personality shine.

◆ Do less but do it well.

◆ Complete leaders select their goals and their battles with care.

◆ Keep it simple: if you don't understand what someone is saying to you they probably don't understand it themselves.

◆ Ethical conduct is the natural partner of drive and ambition.

◆ Be inquisitive.

◆ Take pride in collective achievement.

Tiger Woods won four majors in 2000–2001. To non-sports fans, this is the equivalent of a novelist winning the Nobel, Whitbread, Booker and Pulitzer prizes all in a year; or a business leader achieving record results and picking up three highly prized gongs.

Did the 26-year-old golfing genius give up practising? No. In fact, he carries on practising, perfecting his swing, endlessly rehearsing his putting.

A complete leader who is developing the styles and emotional intelligence that we have described will be seeing strengthened teams and more consistent business performance, and will be better able to cope with economic downturns or other unpleasant shocks. It is never a good idea to imagine that we have 'arrived' and can rest on our oars (if we can be permitted to switch sports for the sake of this metaphor). Complete leadership is a growing process, not a destination.

That's the bad news: the learning never ends. The good news is that the more you learn the easier it is to learn; and the more you learn the better the financial results and the happier the chairman, your spouse and the kids.

Complete leaders select their goals, define the route to them, and equip and motivate their teams to achieve them. They are affected by external shocks, but not slaves to them. Their development and learning, and that of the people who work with them, are simultaneous and mutually supporting. They blend rational analysis with a sophisticated array of behavioural abilities that they have honed in tune with their natural strengths and personalities.

Complete leaders select their goals, define the route to them, and equip and motivate their teams to achieve them.

Heike Bruch and Sumantra Ghoshal, writing in the *Harvard Business Review*, give a succinct summary, using the term 'purposeful managers' where we use complete leaders, to describe a similar level of ability:

'Other managers feel constrained by outside forces: their bosses, their peers, their salaries, their job descriptions. They take all those factors into account when they are deciding what is feasible and what is not. In other words, they work from the outside in. Purposeful managers do the opposite. They decide first what they must achieve and then work to manage the external environment – tapping into resources, building networks, honing skills, broadening their influence – so that, in the end, they meet their goals. A sense of personal volition – the refusal to let other people or organizational constraints set the agenda – is perhaps the subtlest and most important distinction between this group of managers and all the rest.'[29]

Here's an example of a complete leader operating in an interim role for the construction group Arup, as related by Clive Reeder, senior human resources manager at the group:

'He ended up staying with us off and on for two years. He became very supportive for us.

'He used his networking skills around the industry to get us through some major problems with a supplier in a positive way. We were able to challenge the supplier and get a good result. He turned around the situation and the supplier, through his help, began to see us as a better client.

'I was also able to put him up to the board to say things that I couldn't say; and use him to discuss issues and to give me a steer. He was one of us while he was here. He was happy to train our people, for example, in how to set up a spreadsheet and he wouldn't charge separately for that.

'We were stronger when he left, and we have people who are stronger, including me, because of his mentoring and because of the direct training that he provided.'

Complete leadership: let yourself flourish

To be a complete leader means being a rounded person, letting your personality shine, and being aware of how you come across to others. We hope that the excercises in self-awareness and developing managerial styles that we have set out have helped you in some of the core abilities that studies have shown to be associated with high-performing organizations.

Here, we take a look at some of the attributes that can be added to the core disciplines discussed earlier in the book (though doubtless there is some overlap between the two categories).

1 Keep things simple

A common trap for some leaders is to pretend that leadership is terribly complex and requires esoteric analytical methods and opaque language. As we saw in Chapter 2, a business is people: customers buying from your staff. It's easy to have our heads turned by a new fad or piece of terminology, or to be seduced into an acquisition in a sector that is currently trendy (though the collapse of the dotcoms will have corrected this tendency to a degree). Technology is complex, but the principles of business are simple, sometimes brutally so. As Bruch and Ghoshal note, complete leaders do not let their heads be continually turned by external pressures or the multitude of voices of advice that ring in their ears. The best leaders 'pick their goals – and their battles – with far more care than other managers do', they write.[30] Such leaders keep focused on the real customers, the real staff and the core abilities and requirements of the firm. They set their agenda.

Technology is complex, but the principles of business are simple, sometimes brutally so.

Gerry Robinson, former chief executive of Granada, comments:

'Most issues in business require a "nous"-type of judgement which I think is very difficult to learn.

'In fact, I have a feeling that in a way there is an inverse correlation between over-intellectualizing something and the nous for saying "that feels right." I've seen things intellectualized into oblivion.

'If you make mistakes – and probably we all do – it is nearly always because you have allowed your inner feeling to be overcome by a plethora of information which has been presented to you in the most positive way.

'More than anything else leadership requires clarity and simplicity. People like to understand where it is that you are taking an organization and why. They like to understand, and they are more than capable of understanding it too. In fact the first thing to realize is that if you don't understand what someone is saying to you they probably don't understand it themselves. Clarity and simplicity are vital; don't try to do a thousand different things. Have three or four things that you're able to do. It's hardly new, all this, but to really hone down is important. Do less – to do far less is a good adage in business. It's such a temptation to do a hundred things to prove how clever you are and to show how busy you are. Just don't do it – do less and really do the things that you choose to do really well.

'Almost any time I have looked at an organization in trouble it has been trying to do too many things. It's a real temptation. To do less is really, really important and much underestimated. In fact the whole culture is against it. The whole culture is about doing things and always knowing about this and having tested that. Disaster. Do a great deal less should be the norm in most organizations.

'I've worked in organizations where someone at the top today is very excited about project A and two days later is very excited about project B and four days later project C and they just don't understand what that means in terms of the organization swaying under that; trying to find things; trying to back it up; not knowing where they are. At the head of an organization you must ask for very few things because the machine causes its own problems anyway. People are already asking for things down the line. You start swaying around at the top and you just create work. This is often a failure of courage in the first place to say, "No, it doesn't matter how wonderful that looks we're not doing it." So that you cut it off before you have done 57 studies simply out of cowardice.'

2 Be ethical

It's very difficult to shake from the Western psyche the image of the successful business leader as a buccaneer; a ruthless warrior. It's probably all that Francis Drake we did in school. Conquering virgin territory with superior firepower and looting gold for a mediaeval monarch is a poor role model for a leader of a 21st-century business delivering high value-added services with skilled, mobile staff.

It's very difficult to shake from the Western psyche the image of the successful business leader as a buccaneer; a ruthless warrior.

Despite this, military metaphors retain their attraction in the world of business. Maybe this is not all bad. There are inspiring examples of war leaders – from Alexander the Great to Winston Churchill – displaying tremendous leadership skills. But an unfortunate by-product of this thinking is that too many leaders and aspiring leaders go collecting enemies, engaging in gratuitous office politics, imagining that putting someone down increases their power. Success in the modern, globalized, interdependent world requires strong networks of people, and enthusiastic staff following a genuine vision. These are built on trust and honesty.

This was brought clearly to light in the 2001 Hay Group study of entrepreneurs. It found that successful business pioneers scored astonishingly highly on matters of probity and ethics – far higher than the sample of corporate managers also included in the survey.

In the words of the report:

'Well over three-quarters of those interviewed [successful entrepreneurs] displayed high levels of integrity. This means that they are prepared to stick to their principles, even when that might mean taking a financial loss. Entrepreneurs work in an open and highly principled way and are hugely disappointed when others don't play by the same rules . . . [they] foster a culture where ideas are freely expressed, mistakes are openly admitted and people are rewarded based on their individual contribution.'[31]

As we discussed in Chapter 8, being a leader can be likened to being on stage – in the sense that people are watching you – but this doesn't mean acting. We can, and should, emphasize the positive, and refrain from confessing too much about doubts and fears, especially when the business needs to pull itself out of difficult trading conditions. We need to inspire people, and encourage them to identify and build on their strengths. But this does not mean lying. Lies are terribly corrosive to trust, and where trust breaks down, employees, suppliers and the boss cease to have faith in you and, quite simply, cease to work for you. Trust can only be built on integrity.

Perhaps the most significant aspect to the report was the finding that high ethical conduct co-existed naturally with ambition, drive, high standards and visionary leadership. If we have supposed that drive and ambition were automatically opposed to ethics, it's time to think afresh.

3 Be inquisitive

Complete leaders are intellectually curious. They never suppose that they know it all. One study comments:

'Superior chief executives exhibit an underlying curiosity and need to know more about people, things and issues. The result is an awareness of future developments that may create opportunities or avoid problems. One CEO commented: "As you can see, I have reviewed every relevant book and article on the subject of customers. I have spent several years attending a lot of seminars, talks, and discussions on the subject. It has led me to put together my own training seminar. It is not just something that I feel I ought to do. It is something that fires me up".[32]

Superior chief executives exhibit an underlying curiosity and need to know more about people, things and issues.

This attribute is extremely important in terms of technological awareness. Obviously it's not realistic to expect a business leader to be capable of Java programming, but if a modern leader doesn't have a natural inquisitiveness of new inventions, and a close colleague who is technologically literate, he or she is extremely vulnerable to approving the wrong IT system, missing a new product or a new way of doing business.

Frank Lane, a programmer-turned-entrepreneur, runs a design and advertising company in southern England, called Image. He still teaches himself something new about programming every month, as well as avidly reading management textbooks and magazines. As a result of this curiosity, and comfortable with IT, he has introduced the use of WAP mobile Internet technology with his salespeople, at a time when many have been struggling to make the most of the development. His staff can check the availability of advertising space while they are with a client, and book space instantly, connecting to a system that is updated in real time.

Frank Lane describes this relentless curiosity as the habit of being 'permanently in school'.[33] Continual learning means continual inventiveness, which is, as the example above illustrates, a far more effective way of improving efficiency than cost-cutting.

There are indirect benefits also. As we discussed in Chapter 2, the human brain is capable of unknowable improvement, given the right stimuli. One can draw a close analogy with physical exercise improving the body. Run up a hill every morning and our legs strengthen; exercise the grey matter through reading philosophy or playing chess or studying quantum mechanics and our brain capacity improves.

To maintain this capacity, it's important not to become burned out (see page 125). Athletes have discovered that it is possible to over-train – the symptoms are 'muscle soreness and weakness, reduced exercise tolerance, reduced motivation, mood swings, sleep disturbance, recurrent infection, loss of appetite and diarrhoea'.[34]

The same applies to developing the mind; exercise is essential, but overload is dangerous. It's better to consider the quality of our decisions, and gain a sense of the improvements we may have made in our decision-making ability.

4 Take pride in the achievement of others

We can't do everything by ourselves. If you head a large company or division, the vast bulk of the duties and tasks are carried out by others. This is a fairly obvious statement, but the case studies throughout this book have illustrated the ease with which we persuade ourselves that we have to do it all ourselves; and also the achievement and the joy to be gained from letting others shine.

Many of the executives that we've interviewed stress the importance of recruitment: the right person in the right post. If we feel compelled to interfere, then it's possible that we have too much urge to control, and we need to work on this ourselves, but it's equally possible that someone charged with an area of responsibility is simply out of their depth, and would feel enormous relief at being moved to another area, or receiving the training needed to perform well.

The coaching style, as described in Chapter 3, is the one most closely associated with bringing out the best in others, but intriguingly, it's not the only one. Indeed, such is the degree to which achieving your aims depends on others' contributions that the whole of leadership could be said to be creating the climate in which others can shine.

The whole of leadership could be said to be creating the climate in which others can shine.

So, while in the coaching mode you might be directly equipping someone with a new skill, when you are being authoritative or democratic the aim is to empower and inspire, giving people the vision or the space to make the most of their ability. The great thing about the human condition is our endless capacity to improve and to go on learning. This is true of you as a leader, as we hope this book makes clear. It is equally true of every single member of staff whose potential lies dormant in many organizations. Sales staff may be empowered if they learn a new language, or if they are enthused to meet the targets that you set.

In this way, delegation can lead to a multiplication of your feeling of achievement. You have coached Jenny to be a project manager, you have encouraged Luis to step up to the post of finance director, but most of all, your vision and authority inspired the whole organization to improve service, reducing complaints and costs, because everyone wants to serve you and the customers.

Concluding notes

We began this book with the observation that your staff pick up their clues for selecting their behaviour, priorities and tasks from you, the leader; and that behaviour is at least as important as strategy and objectives. We hope you didn't feel paranoid about that, but, rather, curious as to the effect that personal development can have on business success. In turn we hope that this curiosity has led to your cultivation of feedback, and a commitment to the development of self-awareness and leadership skills that we have set out in the preceding chapters. We hope also that this has given you the platform from which to begin to exhibit flair and confidence as you see yourself and those around you succeeding.

The process is simple to conceive, but can be challenging to apply, as we are developing or correcting some deeply rooted behavioural traits. It's a case of strengthening your awareness of how you come across to others; developing the known skills and styles that are associated with success, and applying this knowledge continually. This unlocks the potential of your people.

We hope you are engaged in the journey. Your staff are still watching you. But maybe they are happier with what they see.

notes

1   Lefkowitz, M., Blake, R. R. and Mouton, J. S., 'Status Factors in Pedestrian Violation of Traffic Signals', *Journal of Abnormal and Social Psychology*,1955; see also Cialdini, R., 'The Science of Persuasion' *Scientific American*, February 2001

2   Bloch, S. and Drysdale, J., 'Leadership in New Roles', Hay Group, 2000

3   People Skills Report, Ashridge Management College, June 2002. The top five, in order of rank, were: 1 Communication skills; 2 Influencing (especially without authority); 3 Ability to champion change; 4 Motivational skills; 5 Integrity and trust. The equivalent survey in 1999 had yielded the following order: 1 Communication skills; 2 Motivational skills; 3 Setting and monitoring performance goals; 4 Ability to champion change; 5 Influencing

4   Gabarro, J., *Harvard Business Review*, May–June 1993

5   Bloch, S. and Drysdale. J., 'Leadership in New Roles', Hay Group, 2000

6   www.census.gov/population/socdemo/hh-fam/tabHH-1.txt

7   See, for example, Garratt, S., *Women Managing for the Millennium*, London Harper Business, 1998

8   Hardy, S., 'Small Step or Giant Leap? Towards Gender Equality at Work', policy paper for Work Foundation (formerly Industrial Society), 2001

9   Aram, E. and Noble, D., 'Educating Prospective Managers in the Complexity of Organizational Life', *Management Learning*, Thousand Oaks, September 1999

10 Dreyfus, H. and Dreyfus, S., *Mind Over Machine*, New York Free Press, 1986; and Flyvbjerg, B., *Making Social Science Matter*, Cambridge University Press, 2001

11 Dryden, W. (ed.), *Handbook of Individual Therapy*, Sage Publications, 1996

12 Collins, J., *From Good to Great*, HarperCollins, 2001

13 Cooperrider, D. and Srivastva, S., *Appreciative Management and Leadership*, Jossey Bass, 1990

14 Whitney, D. and Schau, C., 'Appreciative Inquiry: An Innovative Process for Organization Change', *Employment Relations Today*, Spring 1998

15 'Top Teams: Why Some Work and Some Do Not', Hay Group working paper www.haygroup.com/online%5Flibrary/955.html

16 Goleman, D., 'Leadership that Gets Results', *Harvard Business Review*, March–April 2000

17 Byrne, John A., *Chainsaw: The Notorious Career of Al Dunlap in the Era of Profit-at-any-Price*, Harper Business, 1999

18 'Leadership for the 21st Century', Hay Group/LOMA report, 1999

19 Goleman, D., *Emotional Intelligence*, Bloomsbury, 1996

20 Goleman, D., *Primal Leadership*, Chapter 6, Harvard Business Press, 2002

21 Morin, A., 'On a Relation Between Inner Speech and Self-Awareness: Additional Evidence from Brain Studies', *Dynamical Psychology*, 1999, see www.goertzel.org/dynapsyc/1999/morin.html

22 Goleman, D., McKee, A. and Boyatzis, R., 'Primal Leadership: The Hidden Driver of Great Performance', *Harvard Business Review*, December 2001

23 Kegan, R. and Lahey, L., 'The Real Reason People Won't Change', *Harvard Business Review*, November 2001

24 Goleman, D., McKee, A. and Boyatzis, R., 'Primal Leadership: The Hidden Driver of Great Performance', *Harvard Business Review*, December 2001

25 Orwell, G., *Collected Essays*, new edition, Penguin, 1999

26 Bruch, H. and Ghoshal, S., *Beware the Busy Manager*, Harvard Business Press, February 2002

27 www.theschoolofcoaching.com survey results issued by press release in March 2002

28 Caplan, J., '360-Degree Feedback for Performance Appraisal', *Training and Management Development Methods*, 14, 3, 2000

29 Bruch, H. and Ghoshal, S., 'Beware the Busy Manager', *Harvard Business Review*, February 2002

30 Bruch, H. and Ghoshal, S., 'Beware the Busy Manager', *Harvard Business Review*, February 2002

31 'What Makes a Great Entrepreneur?' Hay Group report, 2001

32 *Leadership for the 21st Century*, report by the Hay Group and the Life Insurance Leadership Study, 1996

33 Whiteley, P., 'The Secret of My Success', *Computer Weekly*, 13 September 2001

34 'Over-Training and Infection in Athletes', *Sport England* medical notes, www.sportengland.org/resources/ pdfs/medals/ over_training.pdf

index